# GRAPHO-TYPES

*A new slant on handwriting analysis*

# GRAPHO-TYPES

## The amazing new theory of handwriting analysis that shows how you can change your personality by changing your handwriting

### SHEILA KURTZ
### & MARILYN LESTER

FOREWORD BY SETH FIELDING, M.D.

Crown Publishers, Inc.
New York

*Grateful acknowledgment is hereby given to The New Yorker Magazine, Inc., for permission to reprint the drawing on page 28, copyright © 1982 by Gahan Wilson.*

Published by Crown Publishers, Inc., One Park Avenue, New York, New York 10016 and simultaneously in Canada by General Publishing Company Limited

Manufactured in the United States of America

Library of Congress Cataloging in Publication Data

Kurtz, Sheila.
    Graphotypes: a new slant on handwriting analysis.
    Includes index.
    1. Graphology.   I. Lester, Marilyn   II. Title.
BF891.K83 1983      155.2′82      83-7524
ISBN 0-517-54928-X

Design by Leonard Henderson

10   9   8   7   6   5   4   3   2   1

First Edition

*For Sam*
*You always knew and were always there*

# Contents

# Foreword

In the last decade there has been such a wide acceptance of the science of handwriting analysis among business and medical professionals that I felt compelled to explore it for myself. I found that as a psychiatrist I wasn't alone in believing that handwriting analysis provides an extremely valuable means of assessing human nature.

My colleagues in the scientific community have been conducting research into this field during the last half century with excellent results. Such landmark studies as *Theoretical and Graphological Aspects of Compulsive Illness* (Herbert Binswanger, M.D.) and *Handwriting Analysis as a Psychodiagnostic Tool* (Dr. Ulrich Sonneman) have been extraordinarily important in validating the science of graphology as a method of understanding individual personality.

Handwriting analysis is a powerful key to understanding the nature of human behavior. It is especially useful for a professional like myself who may spend years treating the same patient. Not only is it nondiscriminatory, but it provides immediate, in-depth penetration into an individual's character.

Sheila Kurtz has spent much of her career as a handwriting analyst bringing graphology before the public as a scientific method. Her evaluations have constantly matched mine in reference to patients we have conferred about. I find her cogent analyses an invaluable timesaver in my practice. As a leader in her field, she is not only conscientious but insightful and perceptive as well.

Readers of this book will therefore find themselves part of an exciting discovery, the discovery of one's own power potential. Any technique that helps people learn about themselves and how they interact with other people can only have a positive, enriching effect. *Graphotypes: A New Slant on Handwriting Analysis* is an impressive, stimulating, and provocative way to personal fulfillment.

SETH FIELDING, M.D.

# GRAPHO-TYPES

# 1 A New Slant on Handwriting Analysis

You are about to embark on an adventure—the adventure of getting to know yourself and other people through handwriting. I'll be your guide on this wonderful adventure, and I'll share with you the many insights I've gathered during my career as a handwriting expert and as president of A New Slant, Inc., my New York City-based consulting firm.

We'll take a step-by-step look at your handwriting and we'll develop a simple, clear-cut way for you to analyze your own penmanship. What's more, you'll discover your power potential and talents and learn what personality traits you can use to your own best advantage. You'll learn to excel in the things you want to do the most, be it career, finances, love, or friendship, and you'll explore the options you have available to you in these areas.

You'll understand what works best for you and you'll find out how to cultivate a positive outlook about yourself, even as you're discarding and transforming those traits that may have held you back in the past. In short, you'll be creating a whole new world for yourself.

Your handwriting is one of the most revealing things about you. It's an extension of your self and as much a part of you as any of your physical characteristics. Your handwriting is the means by which you express yourself; it's a record of your personality, reflecting who you are at any given stage.

You may have noticed already that at various times in your life your handwriting has looked different, changing as you have. But what's more astounding is that you can actually change your personality by consciously changing your handwriting! And that's what this book is all about.

I want you to be a better person. I know you can take charge of your life, and so I've devised a series of exercises to help you overcome problems by enhancing positive traits such as self-esteem, confidence, determination, and so on. These exercises appear throughout this book, so by the time you've finished reading it and get to the Personal Inventory in Chapter 9, you'll be well on the way to becoming the new you.

My exercises work and are fun to do. Hundreds of my clients have already benefited from them and now, for the first time ever, I have put them in print. The exercises are easy. Each entails only a few minutes of time in filling up one or two pages with writing of a specific nature.

What makes them work is that you yourself take control. By focusing on specific, positive traits, you are sending messages to your conscious and subconscious mind, reinforcing these positive aspects as part of self. Eventually, your brain gets the message, and your personality accepts these positive changes, casting old fears, problems, or negatives aside.

All in all, by learning some symbols, which I'll show you, and by following my simple step-by-step approach, you'll be able to understand what handwriting analysis is all about. It's as if you were carrying a powerful black box around with you and you never knew what was in it. I'll show you how to open that black box and release the tremendous energy of your potential.

Getting to know yourself and people around you through your handwriting is the key to a new, enriched life, full of abundance and rewards you never dreamed possible. *Graphotypes* will enable you to gain insight into your relationships in all areas of living. This, coupled with your new self-awareness, will give you the ability to score success after success in every facet of your life.

*Graphotypes* can do that for you, and I know, because in my counseling practice I've seen literally hundreds upon hundreds of clients improve their lives with my guidance.

Handwriting analysis, also called *graphology*, is scientific. The pattern of characteristics—potentials, traits, talents, strengths, weaknesses, abilities, emotions, orientations, intellect, values, and physical well-being—that make up the complex human being are all encoded in handwriting every time pen is put to paper.

Handwriting is comprised of many diverse elements—various strokes, such as *i* dots, hooks, *t* bars, and loops—connected together to form letters, words, and sentences.

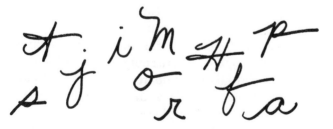

**1.** *Handwriting is comprised of various distinct strokes.*

(See figure 1.) When analyzed, these strokes can be decoded to reveal any and all of the aspects of personality. While graphology does pinpoint behavioral traits, it can't be used to deduce any information of a discriminatory nature, such as your age, race, sex, or national origin. Even the writing of handicapped individuals, who may use their teeth or toes to communicate, can't be discerned as such.

Handwriting analysis is a psychological tool, a scientific assessment method that shouldn't be confused with any of the so-called occult arts such as astrology. Graphology is not predictive; it is a means to evaluate personality accurately as it exists in the present, not in the past or future.

Moreover, graphology is a self-validating science. This means the credibility of the method can be proven immediately by the feedback you get from the graphologist. Validation of handwriting analysis has also come from the scientific community itself. Various comparisons have been made between psychological tests and graphology with the same caliber of information revealed by both. In many cases, in fact, handwriting analysis proved to be more thorough and effective in assessing behavioral patterns than standard psychological tests.

What makes handwriting analysis work is that handwriting is essentially brainwriting. The pen is merely a tool, directed through the movement of your arm by impulses that originate in the cerebral cortex. The message is sent via the nervous system to your arm, hand, and even toe muscles, which motivate the pen to produce the symbols we call writing.

The process is often likened to the action of a seismograph, which picks up signals of earth movement and records them on a graph. Earthquakes can be detected and evaluated in this way. Handwriting records your personality as it is projected through the writing implement.

This has a significant implication—since personalities are unique, so are handwritings. No two, like fingerprints, are exactly the same. However, your writing can and does change to reflect your current personality and outlook on life. Yet the singularity of penmanship is always retained.

On the surface, handwriting styles may appear to be the same, especially among family members. Generally, in such cases, the superficial resemblance is due to a commonality of traits, which are often reinforced in a family or communal structure. Conscious or unconscious attempts to emulate style can always cause a similarity in scripts. The significant differences of personality, however, will always be revealed by a detailed handwriting analysis.

Some superficial characteristics may also be imposed on handwriting because of cultural heritage. Different writing styles are taught in different countries. The essential personality always comes through, though, and the graphologist is able to strip away the nonessentials in order to analyze the basic strokes. The analysis of the basic strokes is also what enables a graphologist to analyze the writing of an individual of any nation that uses the Roman alphabet; the analyst needn't know the language. The strokes are the same in all tongues. (See figure 2.)

2. *This sample is written in Hebrew. The alphabet is not Roman, but many of the strokes can be analyzed for valuable insights into the writer's character.*

Handwriting analysis was known and used by the ancients. Mentions of its use have been found in the texts of the ancient Greek and Roman civilizations. However, it wasn't until the 1600s in Europe, primarily in Italy, that the science of graphology, which had largely remained dormant since ancient times, enjoyed a revival.

Beginning with the seventeenth century, many individuals have researched and furthered handwriting analysis. In the modern era, many of them have been involved in the fields of medicine and psychology. Major strides were made by the French, Germans, Swiss, and Hungarians.

As a result, handwriting analysis has long been an acknowledged science in Europe, often used as a matter of course. For example, in some universities, graphology is a required course of study for those majoring in education or the psychological fields. Some universities even offer degrees in graphology. Businesses in Sweden, Germany, France, Switzerland, and England have long used graphology as an assessment and hiring method.

Such is the popularity and credibility of handwriting analysis in Europe that a Swiss client of mine was led to comment on the state of graphology in the United States. According to this executive: "The United States is ten years ahead of anyone in technology. But when it comes to something as innovative as handwriting analysis I can't understand why this great country lags behind so poorly. We wouldn't think of not using handwriting analysis as an assessment tool."

In the United States, handwriting analysis has, until recently, been used primarily by the law enforcement community. In this regard, one of the most famous cases of the use of graphology occurred in the mid-1930s during the trial of Bruno Hauptmann. Hauptmann was accused of abducting and murdering the infant son of air ace Charles Lindbergh and his wife, Anne Morrow.

Evidence against Hauptmann was inconclusive and the arrest was clouded in controversy. Eventually, handwriting experts were called in, and based on their testimony of analyses of the ransom note compared to Hauptmann's handwriting, the accused was found guilty. Hauptmann was subsequently sent to the electric chair in 1936.

Nowadays, handwriting analysis is used in a variety of applications. For example, medical doctors are using graphology in their diagnostic procedures. The world-famous Strang Clinic in New York City ran a study in the 1970s utilizing handwriting analysis as part of a patient's work-up, which was especially successful in pinpointing cancer and heart disease. However, the program was unfortunately discontinued upon the death of its originator. Other disorders may also be indicated in handwriting samples, such as nervous ailments and alcoholism.

However, medical graphology is an intensely specialized field and even the most seasoned medical graphologists work in alliance with professionals in this area. Since both physical problems and mental disturbances can be detected, these professionals may include M.D.'s, psychiatrists, psychologists, therapists, and so on.

In academic circles, teachers and other educators are awakening to the potential and power of handwriting analysis in assessing the achievement level of students and in helping them to make appropriate career choices.

The major user of handwriting analysis in the United States today is the business community. More than three thousand U.S. companies currently consult handwriting analysts on a regular basis for information on personnel screening, project/departmental/partnership compatibility, options counseling, relocation assessment, outplacement, and promotion evaluation.

Of course, the point is that everyone can benefit from handwriting analysis and can apply this science to almost any life situation. This brings us back full circle to the individual level. You see, your handwriting is so intimately a part of you that you can identify with it, even if you can't relate to what others might tell you about yourself, be they doctors, therapists, or friends.

The best thing about handwriting analysis is that you can do it yourself. You have the power to understand yourself, your relations with others, and to take stock of what you are doing with your life.

As you hold this book in your hands, you stand poised on the threshold of new beginnings. By the time you finish *Graphotypes* you will be on the way to:

• Getting to know yourself better

- Understanding those around you
- Improving your relationships, personal and professional
- Improving your job performance
- Thinking about making changes, perhaps in career or job
- Finding work and personal situations that are compatible with your personality
- Creating new hobbies or interests
- Accentuating the positive things about yourself
- Eliminating the negative things that hold you back.

Throughout *Graphotypes* you will find the specific graphological exercises to help you discover your power potential and develop personality fitness. Paste a sample of your handwriting in a notebook. As you read this book analyze the sample in the context of the points under discussion. Make notes and jot down any thoughts and observations you have. By the time you finish these chapters you will have compiled a very complete, effective picture of your own personality.

You have many directions ahead of you, many possibilities. I'll show you the potentials and paths open before you.

# 2 The Broad Strokes: Basic Techniques I

Handwriting analysis is like putting together a jigsaw puzzle or baking a cake—you need all the pieces or ingredients to create the whole from the parts. And where each part may not mean all that much in itself, the result, your personality, can be thrilling and exciting to unveil. Graphology involves the analysis of hundreds of strokes of handwriting, individually and in relation to one another, in order to see and evaluate a total pattern of behavior.

A sample of handwriting is as complex as the person who wrote it. So you can't tell much by simply glancing at the writing. A detailed study of the strokes is the only way an accurate personality portrait can be painted, so each nuance of the sample must be examined carefully and interpreted circumspectly.

A graphological analysis is so structured that even those who try to disguise their handwriting won't succeed. The true personality always comes through because it's difficult to sustain the concentration needed to truly mask inherent characteristics.

Yet, like medicine, graphology is not only a science but an art. The science comes in mastering the techniques, while the art is in applying those techniques to their best advantage. The combined result is a potent knowledge that will open many doors and can change your life.

## Taking the Handwriting Sample

You don't need many implements to study graphology, but in order to start on the path these few items are necessary:

- A powerful magnifying glass
- Several sharp number two pencils
- A good strong light or (preferably) an artist's light box
- An 8½-by-11-inch bond paper for writing sample
- A legal-size pad of paper for exercises
- Tracing paper
- The GraphoGauge—I'll tell you how to make your own.

First of all, a full page of writing (Fig. 3) is needed to make a useful evaluation. A few words or lines or a signature alone won't provide the quantity of strokes you need to make the assessment meaningful. Therefore, enough writing is requisite to see a pattern emerge and to compare the strokes for consistency.

Never take a sample on lined paper, since the direction the writing takes is significant; lined paper creates a structure that inhibits the writer's natural flow. (See figure 4.) Generally, writing slanting upward indicates optimism, while that slanting downward shows pessimism, so variations from the base line (the imaginary line on which writing rests) shouldn't be ignored.

The author should write anything that comes to mind. The content of the sample doesn't matter because the aim of the evaluation is to analyze strokes, not words or sentences. It should be spontaneous and should be written in a free-flowing, natural style. On no account should the sample be copied, because that, too, would impede the author's ability

Working in New York city is quite an adventure. You meet so many different types of people and are constantly learning, if you keep your eyes open to what is going on around you. I find the idea of handwriting analysis to be fascinating. I feel that any assessment method that can give you additional insights into your personality has to be worthwhile. Possibly through this method you can uncover unused strengths & weaknesses — Anyway here it is.

**3.** *A full page of writing is needed to make a meaningful evaluation.*

to write naturally. The "brainwriting" signal shouldn't be thwarted by the concentration it takes to copy a passage, which breaks up the thought process.

A ballpoint pen is preferable to any other writing instrument for the sample because it gives you the best means to measure the writer's pressure (the way the writer bears down on the paper is significant in an analysis). Fountain pens are also fine, but felt-tipped pens should be avoided unless there is no alternative.

The author should write the sample in any way that's comfortable. The object is to get a sample that completely reflects the personality of the individual who wrote it. If the sample is printed, however, make sure that a few lines of script are added as a backup measure. (See figure 5.) Print-

*The rain in Spain falls mainly*

*The rain in Spain falls mainly*

*The rain in Spain falls mainly*

**4**. *Writing can extend across the page or slant up or down.*

The snow fell with a furry that
I doubted Mother Nature had.
The flakes tumbled hard, striking
the ground one after the other.
In an hour, a thick mat of
white covered the ground and all
on it.

*The blizzard lasted all night and
in the morning we had to dig our
way out of the house.*

**5**. *If a sample is printed, it should always be accompanied by a few lines of script.*

ing can be analyzed in its own right, but the addition of these few lines will ensure that you make a full, accurate analysis.

Once the sample is secured, you're on your way and can begin the evaluation, using the magnifying glass to examine the finer points of the writing.

## Slant

You've probably already noticed that handwritings can slant in different directions. Some people write straight up and down, and others write to the left or far right. This is significant, so your first point of reference is to measure the slant of the script. Slant is the characteristic that shows a person's ability to respond to situations on a feeling level. It's through this capacity for emotional responsiveness that you'll find the key to understanding an individual's temperament and underlying pattern of personality.

Measuring slant is the only mechanical process involved in handwriting analysis. The procedure is easy to master, and is as follows:

1. Take a sheet of tracing paper or clear plastic and copy the GraphoGauge (Fig. 6). A waxy pencil will mark plastic. Set the GraphoGauge aside.

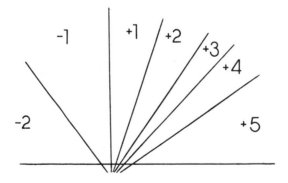

**6.** *The GraphoGauge*

*Meet me in St. Louis*

**7.** *Draw a base line to measure slant.*

*Meet me in St Louis*

**8.** *Sometimes more than one base line must be drawn since every upstroke must be measured from a base line.*

2. Draw a base line under the words being measured (Fig. 7). Since many people do not write exactly straight across, it may be necessary to draw more than one base line under each word (Fig. 8). Make sure that every letter is touching a base line. In order to obtain an accurate picture of the emotional nature, 100 successive lower-case (not capital letters) upstrokes (any stroke drawn up from the base line) must be measured.

**9.** *Draw slant lines up from the base line on upstrokes only.*

3. With a straight edge, draw a slant line on the upstroke (Fig. 9) beginning at the point where the upstroke leaves the base line. Be careful not to measure downstrokes (strokes which return down to the base line—Fig. 10).

4. Take the GraphoGauge and place it over the sample, measuring each of the 100 slant lines individually (Fig. 11). Match up the base line on the GraphoGauge with that on the writing sample. Place the GraphoGauge so the start of the

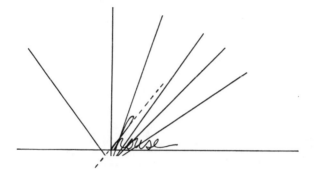

**10**. *Downstrokes are made when the pen returns to the base line.*

**11**. *After slant lines are drawn, measure each with the GraphoGauge.*

upstroke being measured is located at the intersection of the base line and the vertical line.

5. When 100 upstrokes have been measured in this way, calculate the amount of strokes in each section noted, for example, $-2$, $-1$, $+1$, $+2$, $+3$, $+4$, $+5$. The section with the most upstrokes counted will indicate the person's Graphotype. For example, the final count might look like this:

> $+1$  16 strokes
> $+2$  20 strokes
> $+3$  27 strokes
> $+4$  20 strokes
> $+5$  17 strokes

The person is a $+3$ type.

*Note*: If the sample doesn't contain 100 upstrokes, measure as many as possible.

As is shown by the GraphoGauge, the direction of slant can range from −2, extreme backhand, to +5, extremely pitched forward. Each of these areas represents a different kind of emotional responsiveness, which is the basis of what I call the Graphotype personality.

## GRAPHOTYPES: THE SUPRATYPE

If your slant falls in the +1 or +2 range of the Grapho-Gauge you are a Supratype. Your slant varies from vertical to slightly toward the right (Fig. 12). As a Supratype,

*folders are done the way you wanted them. If not, call me or we can make whatever changes tomorrow.*

**12.** *The Supratype writes vertically.*

*Having a wonderful time in this very picturesque spot. The skiing, weather and food have been great. The town, at over*

*Perren-Barberini, Zermatt*

you respond to logic first, prizing thinking and reasoning above emotions, which are put on the back burner when it comes to responding to life situations. Your emotions almost never take over.

Instead, you apply objectivity, evaluating situations with steady, good judgment. You see both sides of an issue and examine all the facts before you make a final decision on the matter. In an emergency, you act quickly and efficiently, keeping your wits about you, reacting emotionally after the emergency is over.

The characteristics of +1 and +2 Supratypes are essentially the same. However, the +2 Supratype is capable of responding more emotionally than the +1 Supratype, who is sympathetic but never impulsive or demonstrative.

13. *Joyce Kilmer, noted poet and journalist, was a Supratype.*

## THE SUPRATYPE PLUS

If your slant falls in the middle area of the GraphoGauge, +3, you are a Supratype Plus personality (Fig. 14).

Barring other trait indications, you are emotionally responsive and empathetic in a temperate manner. Your emotions and reasoning ability are in equilibrium, even though you can act impulsively at times. Supratype Plus individuals possess much expressive energy as well as warmth and outgoingness.

**14.** *People whose slant falls in the +3 area of the GraphoGauge are designated Supratype Plus.*

## THE EXTROTYPE

If your handwriting slants to the far right into the +4 or +5 area of the GraphoGauge you are an Extrotype (Fig. 15).

*repeat Measles vaccine when next in for allergy shot.*

*After five or ten years when I have my degree in psychology and I can give up my present profession, living independently off my interests, my goal in life will have started. Well, at least when I reach a latter age in life, I can say*

**15**. *The Extrotype has a far-right slant.*

Both +4 and +5 Extrotypes share essentially the same quality of emotional responsiveness, but they differ in degree. The characteristics described below are somewhat more intensified for the +5 type.

As an Extrotype you are very emotionally responsive and sympathetic. You are also outgoing and warm and may often be perceived as quite charming. You respond to your emotions first, above all other considerations, and in most situations, apply logic secondarily, unless you have developed controls or other traits in the handwriting to indicate otherwise. (See figure 16.)

Extrotypes possess a great deal of energy and often act impulsively. If other indications are present in the handwriting , the Extrotype personality may be ruled by the emotions or may be unable to control them to the point of being hysterical (Fig. 17).

*thanks for The tea cart. It arrived and I'm delighted with it. What a*

**16**. *This Extrotype has developed a control for emotionalism. It's seen in the arched, umbrellalike t bar.*

*Tomorrow I will go to the Wall Strut office of the company*

**17**. *This Extrotype's slant is so far-leaning as to indicate hysteria.*

## THE INTROTYPE

If you write with a backward slant, −1 or −2 on the GraphoGauge, you are an Introtype (Fig. 18). Again, the characteristics of the −1 and −2 type are basically the same, except that they are intensified for the −2 Introtype.

Introtypes are emotionally withdrawn. If you're an Introtype, you've probably built a wall or a barrier around yourself to guard against hurts, and you may tend not to trust for fear of being injured. As an Introtype you must learn to give to others in order to come out of your shell. You must learn to be communicative and less self-centered. Many performers have backward slants, so their method of extending themselves and reaching out is through their performing (Fig. 19).

Often, backward slants result from childhood incidents. The emotions associated with the incident were never released, turning the individual's emotional focus inward. Introtypes therefore have difficulty in relating to others and lack empathy.

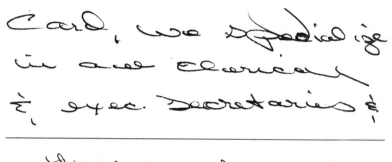

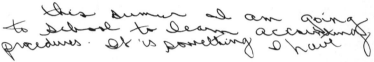

**18.** Introtypes write with a backward slant.

**19.** Bette Davis's slight backward slant may be one reason the great actress went into performing.

The backward slant can be changed, though, and an Introtype can move into the Plus-area of the GraphoGauge. But this can happen only when the Introtype personality releases his or her blocked emotions and learns to relate to others. I'll discuss this in detail later on in this chapter.

## THE VARITYPE

The slant of some people does not fall into any one of the Graphotypes described above (Fig. 20). Their writing is characterized by upstrokes that slant consistently in more than one direction. If this is the case with your writing, you are a Varitype. As a Varitype you are versatile and adaptable and are flexible in emotional situations.

If the writing not only has a variable slant but is erratic—and this is evident in its wild, scattered appearance—the individual can be irresponsible, capricious, and undependable (Fig. 21). Instead of a balanced adaptability to situations, these people behave like the shifting sands, acting differently in the face of similar circumstances. They cannot be counted on to behave reliably.

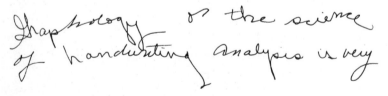

**20**. *Some people write with a varied slant that fits no particular Graphotype.*

**21**. *Sometimes the varied slant becomes erratic, indicating irresponsibility.*

## Pressure

The second consideration in your analysis is the measure of pressure or the amount of force used to press the pen into the paper. Pressure indicates how well individuals react to stress and how stress, in turn, affects them. It also measures energy level, showing how much vitality you put into what you do. Pressure should be equally considered when you evaluate Graphotypes so you can build a complete picture of emotional responsiveness and temperament.

A writer will press into the paper with either light, medium, or heavy pressure. To determine which degree of pressure has been used, turn the paper over and feel the writing from the reverse side. If the paper feels smooth, the writer has used light pressure. If the writing comes through in a pronounced manner, heavy pressure was applied. The gradation in the middle, the slight feel of the writing through the paper, is medium pressure.

A light box is also useful to determine the amount of pressure applied. Gradations of color from light to dark can be clearly seen when the strokes are backlighted. Light shades correspond to light pressure and dark-colored strokes to heavy pressure. There are, of course, degrees in between, indicating medium pressure.

If you write with heavy pressure you have a high energy level, but you also react sharply to stress (Fig. 22); it stays with you and does not fade quickly. People who write with heavy pressure are also the ones to whom environment is very important, as is color and aestheticism, so you require harmony and beauty in your surroundings. You do not function well without it. Beautiful sunsets, artistically presented food, colorful clothes, fine art, breathtaking views, and well-appointed spaces are only a few of the pleasures that are important and necessary to you.

Generally, you are sensuous in your approach to life, and the heavier the pressure, the more sensual the appetites.

*[handwritten sample]*

**22.** The person who writes with heavy pressure reacts sharply to stress.

**23.** Both financier J. Paul Getty and General Lafayette wrote with very heavy pressure.

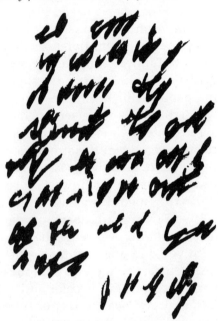

Individuals who write with pressure so heavy that the writing tends to be blotched or muddy have crossed the bounds of sensuousness into varying degrees of sensuality. The muddier the writing, the more primitive the need for sensual gratification. Here, the energy is dissipated into a preoccupation with physical pleasures and a need to gratify the basic instincts of living through food, drink, and sexual encounters.

If you write with light pressure (Fig. 24), you are quite resilient to stress. Whereas your energy level may not be as vital as that of the person who writes with a heavy touch, you are capable of bouncing back very quickly in almost any situation.

And where the heavy-pressure writer puts great gusto into living, plunging in and getting involved (thereby risking the stress that such a life-style invites), you are more blasé. Your live-and-let-live attitude toward life enables you to float through without being too affected by anxiety and stress.

Consequently, you don't get too caught up in your surroundings. This is not to say you don't have a sense of color or environment, but these elements are not as important to you as they are to those who write with heavy pressure.

If you write with medium pressure you fall into the gray area between the two types of writers already mentioned

**24**. *Very light pressure is seen in this sample.*

(Fig. 25). Stress doesn't stay with you for very long. Your energy level is comparatively high and your need for a pleasant, colorful environment is fairly important.

Another important aspect of pressure is that pen choice is related to the amount of pressure applied. Therefore, it's best to write with a pen that accommodates your personality. Choosing a pen is a personal statement, so the selection of a nib or point should be of major concern. (See figure 26.)

For example, if you write with heavy pressure you should use a broad felt-tipped or fountain pen, broad or medium ballpoint pen or number two pencil. If you write with a light touch, you should select a fine-nibbed fountain, felt-tipped, or ballpoint pen and a number three (or higher) pencil.

*why don't you fill them in + I'll get the amount from Philadelphia as soon as*

25. *People who write with medium pressure fall in the gray area between heavy and light.*

*I will send you the memo in the morning*

*I will send you the memo in the morning.*

*I will send you the memo in the morning*

*I will send you the memo in the morning*

*I will send you the memo in the morning.*

26. *Various nibs or points help give the effect of different pressures.*

## Handedness

Are you right-handed or left-handed? Since you are one or the other, you have *handedness*, a term meaning the hand that you naturally use to write. Graphologically, there are no significant differences between left- and right-handed writers. Many people assume that left-handers write with a backward slant, but this is not necessarily true. Grapho-types have nothing to do with handedness and the appropriate slant will come through, even if this means a left-handed writer has to curve the hand in a seemingly uncomfortable way to do it.

It's impossible to determine handedness from a writing sample. The same is true for samples written by ambidextrous people (those who use their right and left hands with equal ease) and the handicapped. In short, there is nothing inherent in the writing itself to indicate the nature of how it was written.

*"It's interesting, you know? You're left-handed and I'm right-handed, and so you make the little cross strokes slant down to the right, whereas I make them slant down to the left."*

27.

## Neat versus Sloppy Writing

Have you ever thought neat people write nicely and sloppy people write badly? Well, the aesthetic "look" of handwriting has a lot to do with the personality of the writer. Scrawled handwriting may look sloppy, but it isn't necessarily indicative of a sloppy or disorganized person (Fig. 28). The reverse is also true: neat writing (Fig. 29) doesn't generally mean its author is neat or well organized.

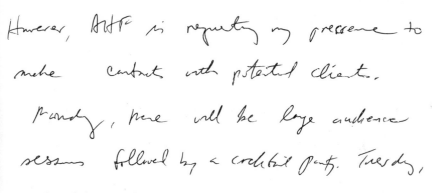

*However, AHP is requesting my presence to make contacts with potential clients.*

*Monday, there will be large audience sessions followed by a cocktail party. Tuesday,*

**28**. *Scrawled writing doesn't mean the writer is messy, just a fast thinker.*

*Handwriting analysis is something I've been interested in for some time. Could you tell me how I can get started and learn how to*

**29**. *This sample of neat writing shows it was written carefully and methodically.*

Scrawled writing means the person thinks faster than his or her ability to put the words on paper. People who write this way may indeed be "messy," but this characteristic may or may not be connected to so-called sloppy writing. You can assume, however, that these people are somewhat undisciplined because they don't take the time to slow down and make their writing more legible.

## Rhythm

Some writing seems to flow across the page without any break in cadence. It's smooth, steady, and unified, and is said to have rhythm (Fig. 30). Rhythm is basically characterized by the fluid motion of the pen across the page and a regular return to the base line, which is consistent and unbroken. In fact, consistency is the key to rhythmic writing and any deviations in it are executed the same way every time. This regularity affects the overall style of writing. The script seems to never break stride.

*The enclosed might be helpful in finding your way around next Friday and Saturday. No word yet on your offer, but I'll contact you as soon as I hear anything.*

**30**. Top: *This sample shows a good sense of rhythm.*

Bottom: *Muhammad Ali's writing lacks rhythm. It was written at a time when he was contemplating leaving boxing.*

*and the Heart is a muscle Burred inside the Breust, The Heart is the Center*

If your writing is rhythmic, it shows stability and a need for some degree of routine. You enjoy taking things on an even keel. In fact, if your routine is disrupted, you probably become upset—because the rhythm of your life has been disturbed.

Too much rhythm can be shown in a sample also. This kind of writing looks mechanical (Fig. 31). It indicates that the writer is mentally rigid and possibly a slave to routine.

The lack of rhythm in a handwriting sample isn't considered negative. This simply means added versatility. An example of rhythm or lack of it can be seen in the effects of a rainy day. Individual A, the rhythmic writer, is accustomed to jogging every morning. Unable to run because of the rain, this person is bored and at loose ends because his or her schedule has been disrupted.

**31**. *When there is too much rhythm the writing looks mechanistic.*

Individual B, whose handwriting lacks rhythm, is also bored, but not for the same reason. This versatile person is at odds with himself or herself only because there is nothing to do; the rain has put a damper on many possibilities for entertainment and enjoyment.

Rhythm is an important key in understanding your own approach to things and how others function on a day-to-day basis. In evaluating personality, rhythm should be considered along with pressure and slant measurements because these traits interact with each other.

## Margins and Spaces

The area left between letters, words, and lines is referred to as spacing, while margins are the borders surrounding the writing. Both contribute to the total effect of the sample. Generally, the more space that's left on a page in margins and elsewhere, the more extravagant the writer (Fig. 32). Conversely, when very little space is left, frugality is indicated (Fig. 33). These are the two extremes, so you can judge the degrees in between.

**32.** So much space is left in margins and between lines as to indicate an extravagant person.

*The wide margins
and full spacings
show a generous
writer.*

Aug 8, 1979

Dear Rose —

Glad to hear
from you! It's
been such a long
time!

We're all doing
great on this end.
Mort and the kids
are in great form —
especially now that
it's the height of

Jack—

We had to go over to Sue's to help with a problem that came up — nothing horrible — you know her — I'll tell you when I get back.

Anyway — I left some veggies, & chicken out to defrost and so if it gets too late or you get hungry — help yourself. I'm going to try to get back as soon as I can, but I wanted to cover the bases, you know!

Remind me to tell you about Angela calling too — interesting!

See you later —

Judy

**33.** *Very little space is left in margins and between letters and lines, indicating frugality.*

Sometimes the writer finds it difficult to maintain an even right margin. In this sample, the writer tries to be frugal, but eventually gives way to a desire to be expansive. The reverse can also happen.

Hi! — I'm just going to drop you a short note because I'm really busy. I heard you just got a little from Cathy anyway, so I bet you have most of the news from her. Forgive me if I repeat anything — I suppose you'll just have to put up with it!

Ok. To start — the reason I'm busy is that I took on a second job. I've decided I've just got to get to Europe this summer & I've built everyone I know has been and I feel like a step child or something! The job is at night, waitressing in your favorite and mine's — Tony's. Can you believe it! I was having dinner there a few weeks ago and on an impulse I asked senior my if he'd hire me. Before I knew it there I was slinging hash on the night shift!

I figure a few months of this should be enough to get me where I want to go.

It doesn't leave me much time for anything else, so I haven't got too much else to tell you, and no time anyway — torn through. Unde to me!

Love

Terri

P.S. [illegible]

*Disorderly margins often reveal disorderliness in the individual. In this sample, the writer shifts between a desire to be thrifty and expansive, and eventually can't resist the urge to fill up the page.*

## The Signature

Your signature is a very intimate part of your handwriting, but graphologically it can't be analyzed for significant personality information. Your signature merely shows certain traits you're projecting at the moment and how you present yourself to the world, regardless of your true Graphotype.

Moreover, your signature can vary, depending on your mood. For example, have you ever gone to a bank and been asked for a signature verification even though you've dealt with that bank for years? Possibly you were in no frame of mind to deal with financial matters that day and your mood was reflected in your signature, which appeared different from the usual one.

People also stylize their signatures according to their self-image. So, while signatures don't reflect the total personality, they do make a statement about how an individual wants to be perceived. When you write your signature, you are issuing a highly individualized statement about you, in essence drawing a statement of projected personality. (See figures 34, 35.)

**34**. *George Washington's signature was stylized, especially in the cross of the* t.

**35**. *Ted Kennedy's signature shows how variable signing a name can be.*

Different writing contexts also cause variations in signatures. You may sign your name differently on a birthday card than a sympathy card, and differently again on a business letter, employment application, credit card form, and so on.

**36.** *The flamboyancy in this sample is very stylized.*

Some people model their signatures, consciously or unconsciously, on those of people they admire, and some use their signatures to project qualities they don't normally have but wish they had. For example, a shy person may have a flamboyant signature full of flourishes and ornamentation that aren't present in the regular writing (Fig. 36). The way you place your name on a document can also be revealing. A prominently displayed signature makes a bold, assertive statement of personality, or, by contrast, it may be inconspicuous, reflecting a desire not to be noticed.

The clarity of the signature is also significant. A clear, readable signature says: "I want to be understood." A person who scrawls his or her signature may be saying just the opposite. Scrawled writing indicates fast thinking, as previously discussed, but when it comes to a signature, it can say, "I don't want you to get to know me."

   Finally, sometimes people underline their signatures as a continuation of the name. This gesture is indicative of self-reliance and confidence; it's a declaration of worth. So any time you underscore your signature, you're reinforcing self-esteem.

**37.** *Former President Jimmy Carter's signature is consistent with his overall style of writing.*

**38.** *What do you think these signatures say about their authors?*

**39.** *Leopold Stokowski, late conductor and composer, and performer Sammy Davis, Jr., have scrawled signatures.*

**40.** *Napoleon Bonaparte's confidence is evidenced in his underscored signature.*

## Changes in Handwriting

As I mentioned in Chapter 1, your handwriting can change in two ways. First, as a reflection of personality, it can alter slowly over time if you make significant changes in your psychological makeup. Second, handwriting can differ superficially from day to day to reflect changes in your mood, attitude, or state of health (Fig. 41). In this latter case, the basic, underlying strokes and traits of personality remain the same, although the style may vary to some degree. For example, the slant may change direction slightly (but within the same Graphotype area), or the writing may divert up or down from your natural base line.

The more sweeping alterations that occur when you make an important life transition are readily seen. (See figure 42.) Your handwriting changes to reflect your state of maturation and awareness, and as you move through the various stages of life, your growth is reflected accordingly. These kinds of changes are particularly noticeable as a child matures and

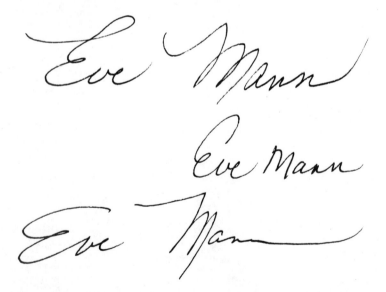

41. *Changes in signature are common, especially when they reflect changes in mood or deliberate stylization.*

Commission on the Review of the Nat'Policy Toward Gambling 1976
FBI crime stats of gambling
Bibliog- Yes You Can Win · Raymond Herkitz , Vantage '69
    Scarnes New Complete Guide to Gamb · John Scarne - Simon & ?
    Fear & Loathing in Las Vegas · Hunter Thompson · Random Hb 70
    To Gamb or Not to Gamb · Walter Wagner · World Pub · 1972

**42**. *Subtle changes are present in the sample* top, *written in 1979* (above), *and written in 1983* (below).

Moving uptown slightly, one
comes to the exciting ethnic areas
of Chinatown and Little Italy. Both
offer a variety of restaurants that
are among the best in the world.

reaches adulthood. But adults tend to settle into a basic pattern of personality, so sweeping changes are only seen if a major attitudinal or psychological transformation occurs.

Furthermore, changes show up in the strokes, not slant, so the Graphotype stays the same—with one exception. An Introtype can become any one of the Plus-area types (Fig. 43). This is because the natural flow of writing is forward, to the right. The bottled-up emotions Introtypes have, as I discussed earlier, turned their writing opposite to the natural flow, just as they are turned inward.

Releasing their inhibitions, be it through counseling, therapy, volunteer work, or whatever, enables Introtypes to reach out. Their focus is redirected externally, and so their slant is able to flow freely forward, reflecting the change.

Plus-area Graphotypes don't change because the slant of writing is forward already, in tune with the natural flow.

The basic emotional makeup remains the same. Significant life changes in Plus Graphotypes are seen exclusively in the alterations of strokes.

**43**. *This Introtype* (above) *became a Supratype* (below) *after several years of therapy.*

## Your Summary Checklist
Here's what you've learned so far:
- *How to take a sample*: Get a full sheet of writing of un-copied material. Ballpoint or fountain pen preferred.
- *Graphotypes*: Found in the slant; gauges the emotional responsiveness. Specific types:
  *Supratype*: emotions under control, logical
  *Supratype Plus*: emotionally temperate
  *Extrotype*: responds to emotions first, impulsive
  *Introtype*: emotionally withdrawn, cautious
  *Varitype*: versatile and adaptable

- *Pressure*: Measures energy level, response to surroundings and stress level. Specifics:
  *Heavy pressure*: high energy, needs colorful environment, affected by stress
  *Medium pressure*: good energy level, pleasant environment important, but can adapt if not present, stress doesn't stay long
  *Light pressure*: lower energy level, not greatly affected by environment or stress
- *Handedness*: Has no bearing on an evaluation.
- *Neat writing*: Does not necessarily indicate a neat person.
- *Scrawled writing*: The person thinks faster than his or her ability to write. Doesn't necessarily indicate a sloppy person.
- *Rhythm*: Flowing writing indicating fluid thought, mental discipline.
- *Margins/Spaces*: Much space left on a page, extravagance; page filled up, frugality.
- *Signatures*: Stylized, individual statement of self-image. Doesn't reflect total personality.
- *Changes in writing*: Occur in two ways—over long term to reflect changes in personality through maturation and growth, and superficially (stylistically) from day to day. Strokes change, not slant, with one exception—Introtype can move into Graphotype Plus-area.

**The Evaluation Process**

You're already well on your way to the thrilling discoveries you'll make through graphology. Here, at the end of the first leg of your journey, I want you to remember that handwriting analysis is an interpretive process based on the evaluation of many elements in the writing sample. In this chapter I've presented some basics and laid the foundation you will use to know yourself and others better.

In the next chapter I'll deal with specifics: the interpretation of the individual strokes of writing. Bear in mind that an accurate assessment of personality can only be made by integrating all the facts. I'll guide you on how to interpret all the elements of writing. Practice will improve your skills.

Also remember that the writer seldom makes the same stroke in exactly the same way, so each sample will show *t*'s, *m*'s, *n*'s, and other strokes written in a variety of ways. (See figure 44.) It's your job then to judge the sample in terms of the preponderance of strokes. That is, you'll have to determine if there are a majority of identical stroke formations. If there's no particular consistency, you should look to the rest of the sample to determine why.

People are comprised of many complex facets of personality, all of which are mirrored in handwriting. You can become adept at interpreting how these many aspects interact with each other, and see the personality unfold before you.

**44**. *In this sample, the writer has made her t's in a variety of ways.*

# 3 Fine Lines: Basic Techniques II

Did you ever stop to think about how many qualities of personality there are? Try making a list—you'll find it's a long one. In fact, in my analyses, I examine three hundred distinct traits in order to arrive at a complete picture of someone's personality. These basic traits are what I use in my business and what I teach in my courses.

Strokes are nothing more than symbols. Each symbol, or stroke, represents a trait of your character, such as persistence, creativity, ambition, goal orientation, dignity, integrity, and so on. The words, sentences, and paragraphs of the sample are unimportant in analyzing handwriting. Decoding the strokes yields the information that you can evaluate and integrate to assess the personality.

## Graphozones

You'll notice first that writing occurs in three planes, located on, above, or below the base line. I call these areas *Graphozones*. Graphozones represent the broad areas within which various traits are categorized.

**45**. *The strokes of writing fall into one of three areas, called Graphozones.*

As figure 45 shows, the Middle Graphozone is the area directly on the base line. The majority of strokes are written here. Although only some letters have strokes that extend up or down, all letters lie in this Graphozone.

Letters with no upper or lower loops are *a, c, e, i, m, n, o, r, s, u, v, w,* and *x*. Their specific symbology in terms of traits will be discussed throughout this book.

The Upper Graphozone contains the upstrokes of the letters *b, d, f, h, k, l,* and *t*. Generally, these Upper Graphozone strokes symbolize traits that deal with an individual's capacity to conceptualize abstract and philosophical ideas.

The Lower Graphozone, containing the downstrokes of the letters *f, g, j, p, q, y,* and *z*, generally symbolizes the creative aspects of personality.

### Thinking Patterns

Graphologically, we all fall into categories called thinking patterns. This means we think either rapidly and comprehensively or more slowly and methodically, building fact on fact to reach a conclusion. Thinking speed has nothing to do with a person's innate intelligence. Rapid or methodical thinkers may be equally as intelligent or well educated, but they simply arrive at conclusions in a different way.

Rapid thinkers make quick encompassing judgments, whereas methodical thinkers need to apply logic to a conclusion. This is not to say that rapid thinkers aren't logical. Rather, their minds work quickly, often so fast that their judgmental process may appear to be almost subconscious.

Your Graphotype doesn't directly affect your thinking patterns. Introtypes, Supratypes, or Extrotypes may all think at the same rate of speed. All may be methodical thinkers, for example. So your emotional responsiveness has little to do directly with the way your mind assimilates information. However, some people develop thinking patterns to complement their Graphotype. For instance, an extreme Extrotype, who is by nature very impulsive, may subconsciously choose a slower thinking pattern to temper his or her impulsiveness.

The strokes that identify thinking patterns are primarily found in the configuration of $m$'s and $n$'s and secondarily in $h$'s. Rapid thinkers make their $m$'s and $n$'s with needlepoints (Fig. 46), which is to say the peak of the $m$ or $n$ is very pointed. Methodical thinkers round the tops of their $m$'s and $n$'s (Fig. 47).

**46**. *Needlepoints*

Analytical thinking is another kind of thinking pattern that is typified by a V formation in either an $m$ or $n$ (or $h$), which touches the base line (Fig. 48). Both rapid and methodical thinkers can have this trait. If you think analytically, you examine problems and situations from all angles and form conclusions about the whole based on the evaluation of the parts.

If your writing has needlepoints, you can perform this kind of analytical thinking almost by second nature. But if you're a mechanical thinker with a natural tendency to mull things over, the V formation will amplify this trait.

An ability to investigate is another thinking pattern found in wedge formations in *m*'s, *n*'s, and *h*'s. Wedges resemble needlepoints but shouldn't be confused with them (Fig. 49). Needlepoints are very pronounced, whereas wedges resemble mountaintops.

*I may go to London.
for one week , then I'll
be home for the winter.
Sam keeps sending*

**47.** *Rounded* m's *and* n's

I would like to mention my favorite scripture John 10:10 "I am come that they might have life, and that they might have it more abundantly." That text applies to your own creative life.

May God grant you good health, peace and joy is my prayer for you.

With friendship and high regard
Cordially, yours
Norman Vincent Peale

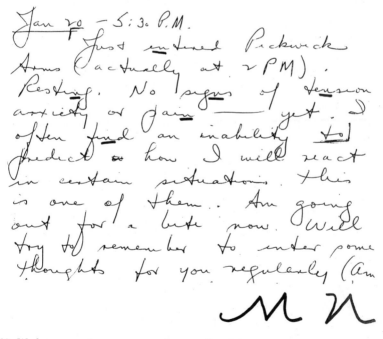

**48.** V formations are evidenced in the writing of theologian Norman Vincent Peale.

Jan 20 — 5:30 P.M. Just entered Pickwick Arms (actually at 2 PM). Resting. No signs of tension anxiety or pain —— yet. I often find an inability to predict how I will react in certain situations. this is one of them. Am going out for a bite now. Will try to remember to enter some thoughts for you regularly (Am

**49.** Wedges are not as pronounced as needlepoints.

Wedges in your writing indicate that you are good at research and enjoy searching for answers. You seek out your own sources of information and make decisions and form conclusions based on this exclusive input.

The size of the wedge measures your ability and potential to investigate issues (Fig. 50). The larger the wedge, the greater your capacity to investigate and get to the root of the situation. On the other hand, small wedges show that the person, although inquisitive, isn't deeply concerned about the great implications of an issue, and finds surface information to be sufficient.

The absence of the V formations or wedges in *m*'s, *n*'s, and *h*'s indicates that the upstrokes of these letters have been retraced. Retracing means drawing over any stroke that's already been written. While retracing is commonly found in *m*'s, *n*'s, and *h*'s, they can appear in *any* letter (Fig. 51). Generally, people who retrace letters are repressing thoughts, feelings, or emotions.

When retracing is found, specifically in *m*'s, *n*'s, and *h*'s, it means that the writer is retarding the efficiency of his or her thought process by holding back. If you retrace, you might want to experience more self-expression and work toward opening up more.

**50**. *Wedges can vary in size.*

**51**. *Retracing strokes isn't confined to* m's *and* n's.

$M$'s or $n$'s that are ill-formed indicate an incapacity for deep thought. Usually, this person writes with a severe scrawl, rendering these letters almost illegible (Fig. 52). People who write this way have a tendency to skirt issues and to consider only the shallow, superficial areas of thought. If you come across such writing you should look at other strokes to determine what traits may be affecting this thinking pattern.

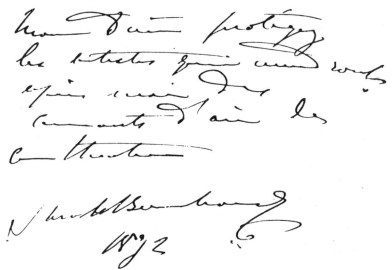

52. *Sarah Bernhardt's scrawled writing especially shows how* m's *and* n's *can be almost obliterated.*

## Direction

As I've suggested before, when you write you move your pen across the page with a positive, forward thrust, so the letters and words flow naturally from one to the other. The writing is progressive, acknowledging movement ahead, into the future. Because forward motion (Fig. 53) is the accepted norm, strokes that don't carry through this way represent attitudes of the past. Again, Introtypes are a prime example of looking back, since all their strokes are slanting left, usually as a result of unreleased childhood traumas.

All formations carried back are called *back-to-self strokes* and are indicative of living to some degree in the past. That degree depends on the frequency with which back-to-self strokes show up in the sample. (See figure 54.)

Typically, these strokes appear at the end of words and are brought up and back to the left, but they can manifest in any number of letter formations throughout the writing.

**53**. *Forward-moving handwriting*

**54**. *Individual strokes can be written back to self rather than forward. James Earl Ray's writing shows this clearly.*

## Corrugated Writing

Are you under the impression that writing gets shaky with old age? If you are, you're mistaken. Writing can be shaky at any age, and many oldsters write as steadily as they did when they were young.

Shaky, spidery script is called *corrugated writing*, and although it's erroneously associated with age, it's actually the result of physical illness, mental disturbance, or severe upset. (See figure 55.) The actual source of the corrugations is difficult to pinpoint in a sample. It takes much practice and experience.

Corrugations may be obvious, or they may be so subtle as to be seen only with the aid of your magnifying glass (Fig. 56). When you're examining a sample, even if it seems fine, make a routine check for corrugations.

55. *Heavily corrugated writing*

56. *Corrugations can sometimes be subtle.*

## T Strokes

More than any other letter in the Roman alphabet, the *t*, both bar and stem, gives you the most opportunity to use any number of different strokes. Any one sample will invariably contain a variety of *t* formations, reflecting different aspects of personality. In fact, *t*'s reveal more about you than any other single letter or stroke.

The placement of the bar on the stem represents goal orientation. The higher the bar on the stem, the higher the goals are placed. If your goals are low, your *t* bar will cross the stem very low. If you have practical goals, the bar is crossed at the middle of the stem. The following illustrate significant *t* bars:

The bar floats over the stem. This individual has very high goals but is a dreamer who may never make those visions come true unless good achievement traits are found in the rest of the writing.

57.

The bar rests on the stem. Goals are placed very high. The writer is ambitious, with the practicality to put ideals into motion.

58.

The bar crosses the stem near the top. Goals are considered well placed.

59.

The bar crosses the stem in the middle. Practical goals are indicated.

60.

The bar crosses the stem near the bottom. Goal orientation is low.

61.

The sweep of the *t* bar shows your level of enthusiasm (Fig. 62). The longer the bar sweeps from the left of the stem

*The boast of heraldy of pomp and power*

*all that beauty, all that wealth ere gave*

*alike await the inevitable hour*

*the path of glory leads but to the grave*

*Thomas A Edison*

**62**. *Thomas Alva Edison's t bars show great enthusiasm.*

to the right, the more enthusiasm you put into living. Pressure enters into the evaluation also; the heavier the pressure on the bar the more enthusiasm is enhanced. Ergo:

Sweeping *t* bar + Heavy *t* bar pressure = Great enthusiasm

The *t* bar is indicative of many other traits as well. The following show the more significant *t* bars:

The bar made to the left of the stem shows procrastination.

**63**.

The bar made to the right of the stem shows temper.

**64**.

The bar slants up, showing a positive attitude.

**65**.

An arrow-shaped bar indicates sarcasm.

66.

The bar slants down to the right with a blunt tip, indicating obstinacy or domination.

67.

A slant down to the right with an arrow shows the writer is domineering.

68.

The bar slants down on the left of the stem, showing that the person is harshly self-critical.

69.

The bar written as a cup means the person is shallow in purpose.

70.

The bar that looks like an umbrella shows the writer is trying hard to keep something under control.

71.

The bar that starts thick and becomes thin indicates slackening willpower.

72.

The absence of the bar altogether shows a lack of attention to details.

73.

The *t* stem is as informative as the *t* bar. The following give some of the more important stem configurations.

The rounded stem shows a deliberate personality, the individual who takes time and doesn't jump into things.

74.

The tentlike stem indicates stubbornness.

75.

The retraced stem shows repression.

76.

The stem is made into a loop, showing sensitivity to criticism.

77.

The tall stem, which is about two times higher than the letters in the Middle Graphozone, shows pride. The writer also wants to be held in high esteem and needs approval from others.

78.

The very tall stem, three or four times the height of letters in the Middle Graphozone, indicates vanity. Pride has turned into vanity because these people have not earned the esteem of others, nor have they reached their own goals. As a result, they exaggerate their abilities and attainments to everyone.

79.

### I Dots

Your ability to pay attention to details is found in the way you dot your *i*'s. The closer the dot is to the stem of the *i*, the better you can handle detailed work. Conversely, dots placed high above the stem, or away from it, toward the right, show you aren't detail minded.

The following show the significance of various *i* dots:

The well-placed dot indicates good attention to details.

80.

The "traveling" dot shows the person is less attentive to working with details.

81.

No dot at all indicates a total lack of enthusiasm for details. Check other traits to see if organizational ability, concentration, or some other compensating trait is present.

82.

The rounded dot indicates loyalty.

83.

The slashed dot shows the writer is irritable over having to cope with details, especially if he or she must sit for long periods of time doing such work. *Note*: not all slashed *i* dots are apparent to the naked eye. Use a magnifying glass to check.

84.

The dot that is a circle is idiosyncratic; it's a conscious gesture to be different.

85.

### Upper Loops

Upper loops extend into the Upper Graphozone, which represents your ability to conceptualize.

Specifically, the upper loops of the letters *b*, *h*, and *l* pertain to your interest in and capacity for philosophical/

religious thoughts. They measure how much imagination you have in these areas.

Basically, the fuller the loop (Fig. 86), the more intense your interest in philosophy/religion/mysticism, and the greater your ability to think abstractly. However, the absence of upper loops doesn't necessarily mean you have no religious or spiritual values whatsoever. Other factors in the writing may compensate.

When the *t* stem is made into a loop, or when the upper loop on the letter *d* is inflated, the writer is sensitive to criticism (Fig. 87).

86. The upper loops in this sample are well developed.

87. Loops in the d and t stems show sensitivity to criticism.

## Lower Loops

Lower loops fall into the Lower Graphozone, which deals with imagination and creativity.

Specifically, the lower loops of the letters *g, j, y,* and *z* are a measure of your creative and/or imaginative potential. Inflated, but not exaggerated, lower loops indicate you possess creativity and imagination (Fig. 88). Those potentials diminish as the loop compresses and becomes a line. People who make no lower loops are practical (Fig. 89); they understand best what they can see and touch. Very exaggerated lower loops, on the other hand, show that imagination has crossed into the realm of exaggeration and overstatement (Fig. 90).

**88.** *Joan Crawford's inflated lower loops show creativity and imagination.*

Narrow lower loops also indicate selectivity in friend-ships. The wider the loop, the more people you want to involve in your life. The person who makes no loops is a loner.

When analyzing loops, look to see if they touch the base line on the upstroke (Fig. 91). If the loop doesn't, it generally means the writer has no follow-through.

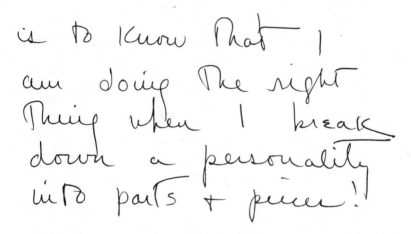

**89.** *There are few loops in this sample, showing a factual approach to life.*

**90.** *Very large lower loops show exaggerated imagination.*

**91**. *The lower loops in this sample do not return to the base line.*

## The Letter **P**

The lower loop, or stem, of the lower-case *p* has a unique meaning pertaining to your desire for physical activity. The more the stem is inflated, the greater the desire (Fig. 92). Handicapped individuals often show this trait.

If there is no loop whatsoever (Fig. 93), two meanings may be drawn: either the writer is content to be physically inactive or he or she is intensely active and desires no additional activity. Many athletes write their *p* stems without loops. This is especially true of athletes involved in sports that require precision, where the retraced *p* stem indicates good timing ability (Fig. 94).

*We had such a good time*
*Thurs might Your apartment*

**92.** *This sample shows a desire for physical activity.*

*In to find out if my present professional interest*
*compatible to certain important variables of my*
*personality through your analysis.*

**93.** *The desire for physical activity in this sample is not very pronounced.*

*one sacrament of life.*
*7. Take time to help and enjo*
*it is the source of hap*

**94.** *This is the precision p—it is retraced.*

### The Letter **F**

Like the *p*, the loops of the letter *f* have a singular meaning. Both upper and lower loops measure your organizational ability. Generally, a well-formed *f* (Fig. 95) shows good organizational ability with a capacity to be flexible.

Loops that aren't in balance show a diminished organizational ability, the degree of which depends on the severity of the imbalance. An ill-formed *f*, for example, indicates very poor organizational skills.

*Basically my problem is that I feel that I have not really*

**95**. *This sample shows a well-formed, balanced* f.

Keep in mind, too, that there are different kinds of organization. You can have a very organized mind and a cluttered desk at the same time (good *f*'s with analytical thinking patterns), so it's important to compare traits like these to see where specific organizational abilities lie.

## Other Loops

There are a variety of loops incorporated into the other letters of the alphabet, each with its own special meaning.

The following illustrate some of the more important miscellaneous loops:

The larger the loop on a capital *I* or *J*, the more responsibility you can or want to handle.

96.

Small loops in letters, especially in *m*'s and *n*'s, indicate jealousy. Large loops indicate that jealousy has been overcome. Without jealousy, the individual is ready to assume responsibility—so the small jealousy loop turns into the large responsibility loop.

97.

Inside loops made on the left side of *a*'s and *o*'s indicate self-deceit.

98.

Inside loops made on the right side of *a*'s and *o*'s indicate secrecy.

99. *O arent over*

Inside loops made on both sides of *a*'s and *o*'s are called *double loops*. They indicate deception. The deception can be of any nature, ranging from an unrealistic Pollyanna-like view of the world to base lying and cheating. For example, doctors and lawyers often have double loops in their handwriting, reflecting the fact that they frequently choose to hold back information as part of their professions.

100. *O ask ore*

## Hooks

Hooks, as the name implies, are little fishhooklike marks that can appear either on the initial strokes of a letter or on final strokes (Figs. 101, 102).

Hooks can't always be seen by the naked eye. Often, they can only be detected with the aid of a magnifying glass.

Initial hooks, hooks found at the start of a word, are a mark of acquisitiveness, monetarily or otherwise—for example, the acquisition of knowledge or friends. Many small hooks indicate that the person likes to acquire many small things. He or she may be a grasping type, however, but this will be corroborated by other traits in the sample.

As the hooks become larger in size, so do the acquisitions the person is interested in obtaining. Collectors often have hooks in their writing (Fig. 103).

Final hooks, appearing at the ends of words (Fig. 104), indicate tenacity, or the quality of holding on tightly and not letting go of what you believe in. If there are many final hooks in the sample, the person is strongly tenacious. The traits of acquisition and tenacity are frequently found together in the same sample.

*Many    hat*

*Cow      Book    cutensil*

**101**. *Initial hooks can be written on many letters.*

*M  em  M  m  M*
*M   m   m*

**102**. *Initial hooks can be large or small and subtle.*

*Let's talk about articles that help people find themselves and make them selves happier. It all goes too quickly*

**103.** *The initial hooks in this sample show a collector.*

*American Football is a source of constant delight for me, outwardly it seems brutal compared to my particular favourite sport, soccer, but on further observation its a game*

**104**. *Many of the final hooks in this sample need to be seen with a magnifying glass.*

## Final Strokes

Strokes that end words are called *final strokes*. The following show some common final strokes:

Short firm finals indicate decisiveness.  105. *decisive*

Long finals mean generosity, especially if the final strokes are combined with wide margins.  106. *generosity*

Finals that curl under and underscore the word to some extent mean self-reliance.  107. *underscore*

Finals that ascend high and to the right indicate a desire for attention.  108. *attention*

Finals that descend to the right indicate pessimism or depression.  109. *pessimism*

The final that breaks away shows initiative.  110. *split*

A long final that shoots straight out to form a line shows caution or prudence.  111. *caution*

When the final sweeps up and over the word, self-castigation is indicated. The backward stroke shows the writer may blame himself or herself for things that happened in the past. A preponderance of these strokes means the person is mired in the past.  112. *Castigation*

If the final doesn't sweep back, but merely touches the preceding letter, self-reproach is shown.  113. *reproach*

## Capital Letters

Although the main thrust of interpretation in graphology is in the small letters, capitals also have their own significance.

Printed capitals, for example, indicate simplicity of personal style or an artistic nature (Fig. 114). Big capitals (Fig.

115) show that the writer has a good deal of self-esteem. Self-confidence is shown in the capital *T*; here (Fig. 116) the letter is tall, with the bar well placed on the top of the stem.

When there's an ink blot on the initial stroke of a capital letter (Fig. 117), the person is hesitant; he or she may fear starting anything. Capital *I*'s that are written so large as to be out of proportion with the script indicate egotism. Conversely, capital *I*'s that are the same size or smaller than lower-case letters show a lack of confidence (Fig. 118).

**114**. *Printed capitals along with script*

**115.**

**116.**

**117.**

**118.**

## Miscellaneous Strokes

There are a variety of other strokes, not classified above, that are indicative of important personality traits. The following show many of them:

A short, straight initial stroke, forming a right angle to a downstroke, is called a *temper tick*. As the name implies, it shows that a person's temper is easily aroused.

**119.**

The tie stroke means the writer is persistent.

120.

Flourished initial strokes, usually in *m*'s and *n*'s, show a sense of humor.

121.

Knots are strokes caused by additional pressure on the pen; they indicate hesitation.

122.

Many flourishes and ornamentations indicate the person has flair. When ornamentations become excessive, however, the quality descends into ostentation.

123.

Breaks between small letters signify intuitive abilities; the more breaks, the greater the intuition.

124.

## Controls

If you haven't already noticed in your own handwriting, sooner or later you'll come across a sample that shows one or more traits that are opposite to each other. Often one trait is positive and the other negative, such as caution and impulsiveness.

What has happened is that the person has developed a second trait that compensates for the negative aspect of the first. Such a counterbalance is called a *control*. Thus, caution becomes a control for impulsiveness. Controls can be expressed like this:

Caution + Impulsiveness = Balance

Caution is only one of several common control traits apparent in some samples. Other typical controls are: the umbrellalike *t* bar, trying to keep the lid on something; needlepoints, comprehension; rounded *m*'s and *n*'s, logic; V formations, analytic ability; vertical slant, emotional control; tall *t* stems, pride; and retraced *t*'s and *d*'s, dignity (Fig. 125). Be sure to check the writing for controls when you're doing an analysis.

*At the height of the winter season, attendance numbers about 200. There's*

*tar dart*

**125**. *Dignity is seen in retraced* t *and* d *stems.*

## Your Summary Checklist

Here are the highlights of this chapter:

- *Graphozones*: The three planes where writing occurs in relation to the base line (page 45–46).
- *Thinking patterns*: Approaches to thought found in *m*'s and *n*'s. *Rapid thinkers* have needlepoints; *methodical thinkers* have round *m*'s and *n*'s; *analytical thinkers* have V formations; *investigative thinkers* have wedges (pages 46–51).
- *Direction*: Writing that doesn't move forward, which is the norm, indicates living in the past (pages 51–52).
- *Corrugated writing*: Shaky writing is indicative of physical illness, mental disturbance, or severe upset (pages 52–53).
- T *bars*: Show goal orientation, enthusiasm level, and a variety of other traits listed on pages 54–56.
- T *stems*: Show a plethora of different traits, listed on pages 56–57.
- I *dots*: Indicative of ability to pay attention to details (pages 57–58).
- *Upper loops*: Show capacity for abstract thought (pages 58–59).

- *Lower loops*: Show capacity for creativity and imagination, as well as selectivity in friendships (pages 60–62).
- P *stems*: Measure a person's desire for physical activity, as shown on pages 62–63.
- F *loops*: Indicative of organizational ability, as shown on pages 63–64.
- *Other loops*: A miscellany of traits catalogued on pages 64–65.
- *Initial hooks*: Desire to acquire things (pages 65–66).
- *Final hooks*: Tenacity (pages 65–66).
- *Final strokes*: Indicative of many different traits, shown on page 67.
- *Capitals*: A variety of meanings as shown on pages 67–68.
- *Miscellaneous*: A catalogue of strokes of various meaning on pages 68–69.
- *Controls*: Certain traits incorporated into the personality to balance the effects of other opposite, negative traits (pages 69–70).

**The Evaluation Process**

Now that I've shown you most of the basic strokes of handwriting, you're ready to make some exciting explorations and to start fully examining the traits individually and in concert with each other.

You'll also begin to see how the Graphotypes fit in with the various traits, so your notebook should be chockful of new discoveries about yourself! As you read on you'll be adding to your storehouse of knowledge by doing the exercises and learning still more traits. Your analyses will become even more complete and sophisticated.

By the time you reach the final chapter, you'll have a comprehensive picture of your own personality, which I'll help you put together by guiding you through the Graphoprofile, your own personal inventory. But for now, as you go on, you'll see how you can make handwriting analysis work for you in your everyday life.

# 4 Projecting Yourself to the World

At 7:30 A.M. John Keenan* rose from a sound sleep and prepared himself for the day. During the course of dressing, he convinced his wife to see a certain movie with him that evening and spoke sharply to his youngest child about her poor school grades.

At 9:00 he arrived at his job as a purchasing manager in a small manufacturing firm, comfortably settling into the day's routine. Before lunch he'd already made several important decisions and persuaded his superior to allow him to try a controversial new vendor.

Mr. Keenan's lunch hour was spent pleasantly with two co-workers in the company cafeteria. The conversation ranged from the weather to baseball to the work routine to politics. Mr. Keenan put forth some very definite opinions on all subjects, and he met with some heated debate over his favorite candidates in the upcoming local election.

*All names in *Graphotypes* have been changed as a matter of confidentiality.

On the way home, he stopped at the dry cleaners, only to find out that a pair of trousers was missing. At first the cleaning establishment didn't want to take responsibility for the mistake, but eventually an agreement was reached.

Home once again, Mr. Keenan relaxed before dinner by having a bout with his son on the electronic video game console, but not before a challenge from John, Jr., on the merits of another game that he preferred to play. Dinner was the usual round of family conversation, and eventually Mr. Keenan enjoyed the movie he had convinced his wife to see that morning.

Mr. Keenan's day sounds pleasant, if not routine. Perhaps you think it wasn't very dynamic at all. But in point of fact, that's not true, for throughout the course of the day, Mr. Keenan was actively and energetically involved in selling himself. How? By projecting himself in his world. Let's briefly go through his day again and observe Mr. Keenan, the salesman:

| | |
|---|---|
| • Convinced wife re: movie | Sales |
| • Urged daughter to get better grades | Sales |
| • Persuaded superior re: vendor | Sales |
| • Put forth his views at lunch very strongly | Sales |
| • Haggled with dry cleaner | Sales |
| • Convinced son to play certain video game | Sales |
| • Presided at family dinner table; gave advice and opinions | Sales |

We're all continually selling ourselves throughout the course of every day, which means we're projecting ourselves in our environment from moment to moment. As we see from Mr. Keenan's example, the ability to project oneself to the world doesn't belong exclusively to a professional salesperson.

## Selling Yourself

Selling yourself on a daily basis in areas such as interpersonal relationships and at work really means you're selling your personality. You can't avoid sales; it's inherent in living. Sooner or later everyone is called on to make a sale of one sort or another.

Selling yourself is intertwined with your self-image, so if you're able to project yourself successfully, you've got a good deal of positive energy that helps you go after and get what you want. (See figure 126.) Conversely, if your self-esteem is low, you won't be able to get what you want—you won't make the sale.

**126.** Top: *The writing of Calvin Coolidge shows good self-esteem, especially in the high t bars and large capital letters.*

Bottom: *John Wayne's writing also shows self-esteem.*

One of the most profound ways in which we are involved in personal sales is in establishing interpersonal relationships, especially in love. Meeting someone and making contact is nothing but salesmanship. Here are two approaches:

Evans Riese is a shy middle-aged man who's already been married and divorced. Over the years he's fallen into a routine which includes plenty of reading, jogging to keep fit, and chess one night a week with an older male friend. Occasionally he will date someone, but generally these are established friends. He's had one or two short affairs since his divorce, but he hasn't been sexually involved in over a year. (See figure 127.)

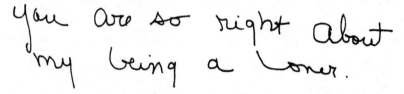

127. *The lack of loops in y's and g's and closed a's and o's (reticence) show Mr. Riese, a Supratype, to be a loner.*

Recently, a friend convinced him to attend a party at the home of someone he didn't know. He was reluctant to go, spent most of his time in a corner, and left early.

At one point in the evening, Mr. Riese was introduced to a young woman whom he found attractive. He would have liked to pursue her, but he was at a loss for conversation, and eventually her attention was drawn to another group of people.

Joe Forlini was at the same party. He, too, is a divorced man in his early forties. Mr. Forlini has always been outgoing, and after the trauma of his divorce passed, he resumed an active social life that includes many friends and casual and serious dating. (See figure 128.)

Joe Forlini was also introduced to the girl Evans Riese found attractive, and he, too, was captivated by her. He engaged her attention by drawing her out in conversation. He displayed a genuine interest in her aside from the possibility of a sexual relationship, and, as a result, she consented to go out with him.

Obviously, Joe Forlini was successful where Evans Riese wasn't, for the simple reason that Mr. Forlini effectively sold his personality to the young lady. Feeling self-confident and being able to put yourself across, no matter what the situation, are important ingredients for successfully projecting yourself to the world. So is determination, or else you'll give up before you reach your goal. (See figure 129.)

**128.** Mr. Forlini's writing shows enthusiasm (swept t bars) and talkativeness (open o's and a's).

*all I could find - hope it's satisfactory .*

**129**. *Determination is seen in the long firm downstroke of the lower loop letters.*

You're now going to embark on what makes this book unique and what can turn your life around—the grapholog-ical exercises I've devised for you.

The beauty of these exercises is that you can do them yourself without a professional. They are clear and easy and tremendously effective. You'll be exhilarated to see the posi-tive changes in your personality after doing them for a short time.

These exercises work because they help you focus on a desired trait, sending positive signals to the brain. Eventu-ally, your subconscious gets the message and the result is that you incorporate this positive trait into your personality.

*Note*: These graphological exercises appear throughout the following chapters. Apply the method given below to each. During and after each exercise, examine your reactions and feelings by recording them in your notebook. Also make sure you try to relate and carry through these exercises to your daily activities.

THE METHOD

When doing the following exercises, make sure that you're comfortable. Maintain the natural tempo of your writing even as you are deliberately making changes. Do one exercise at a time, daily, for at least a week. If a word or sentence is involved, choose one that's pleasing to you.

## EXERCISE FOR SELF-ESTEEM

On your legal-size pad, write your name over and over across the page, underscoring your name every time, as shown in figure 130. Fill up to two pages in this manner. Do the same thing when you write your signature in your day-to-day routine. Every underscore consciously reinforces your concept of self-worth.

**130.**

## EXERCISE TO IMPROVE DETERMINATION

Choose a short sentence with the word *determination* in it and write it over and over across a legal-size sheet of paper, filling up one or two pages. Make sure all the downstrokes are straight and firm, which is the trait for determination (Fig. 131).

**131.**

Since determination is the same as follow-through, you shouldn't stop at this exercise alone. Follow through by consciously applying this trait in your day-to-day writing until it becomes part of you.

### Fear Traits

Often, people who aren't good at projecting themselves are blocked by fears. These fears can vary, but their common denominator is that they prevent the person from achieving desired goals.

The three basic fears from which the others spring are: (1) the fear of losing equilibrium (control), (2) the fear of failure or exposure (fear of being found out), and (3) the fear of disregard. All fear traits can be placed in one of these categories. Graphologically, fear traits are characteristics that develop as a result of these three basic fears.

Some of the common fear traits have already been described, such as sensitivity to criticism (loops in *t* and *d* stems), repression (retraced strokes), desire for attention (long, high final strokes), self-castigation (finals turned backward), withdrawal (backward slant), jealousy (tiny loops in initial *m* and *n* strokes), and procrastination (*t* bar made to left of stem only). Self-consciousness is another fear trait, indicated in the letter *m* when the second hump of the *m* is larger than the first (Fig. 132).

Curiously, in my experience, I've seen some very successful business men and women with quite a few fear traits in their handwriting. What's also present in the handwriting is the will to overcome these fears and succeed. This is shown by the development of controls and may include any of the specific control traits discussed in the preceding chapter or any positive traits such as assertion, persistence, or good goal orientation. In any case, obstacles have to be overcome or controls developed before you can successfully sell your personality and effectively project yourself to the world. (See figure 133.)

**132.** *When the second hump of the* m *is larger, self-consciousness is indicated.*

**133.** *Charles Darwin is one who developed very strong controls, seen in the umbrellalike* t *bars.*

## Options Counseling

A major part of my business at A New Slant, Inc., is in options counseling. Everyone has choices, no matter what the situation, and through the insights I get with handwriting analysis, I'm able to show my clients just what those choices are. No one has to be stuck—you *can* take charge of your life!

Options counseling is for people who want to make a change and project themselves in the best way possible. I'm sure you already know that making changes is seldom an easy task, especially when they involve a major life issue, such as career, vocation, or relationships. Unfortunately, all too often people remain in situations that are no longer appropriate for them, or that they never really enjoyed to begin with, or that they have come to dislike.

The reason is that people often fear change; in the midst of a crisis they become narrow-sighted and frightened and get stuck in their tracks. The result: they fail to realize there are options open to them, and they lose the ability to sell themselves.

We all go through unavoidable changes at various times in our lives. Sometimes they're easy to make (especially if we've actually initiated the change), and sometimes they're painful or confusing. It's important for you to be aware of the situation you're moving through. Self-awareness greatly reduces the stress you feel in life-change situations and helps make change a positive rather than an anxious experience.

When you're at a crossroads it's also extremely important to project a positive attitude (Fig. 134). It's helpful to actually visualize yourself in positive situations. When you do, not only do you reinforce the fact that options are open to you, but you also train yourself to view yourself as a success—and you are!

Attitude makes all the difference. Filling yourself with negativity is tantamount to gearing yourself to lose; you'll inevitably make failure a foregone conclusion. And who wants that? If you don't feel or believe there are options for you, then attitude is something you have to work on.

The exercises throughout *Graphotypes* are aimed at helping you improve your attitude. Take advantage of them! Also, check your handwriting for signs of negativity or pessimism (Fig. 135). For example, are the final strokes moving

*Hope this is some help. I'm writing this standing in the line at the post office — Les*

**134**. *This sample shows optimism, indicated by the upward slope of the lines and t bars.*

*I AM A SHORT STORY WRITER WHO THINKS HE WILL BE NEEDING AN EDITOR.*

*AS YET I HAVE NO WORK OVER 5,000 WDS.*

*PLEASE REPLY WITH INFO + RATES.*

**135**. *The general sloping down of lines and strokes shows pessimism.*

back into the past or drooping down significantly (Fig. 136)? By the same token, are the lines of writing themselves sloping downward? If you see any of these signs in your handwriting, concentrate on the following two exercises, which are especially designed to encourage a positive attitude.

## EXERCISE FOR OPTIMISM

As usual, fill up a page or two of legal-size paper; choose a word or short sentence and start by writing a few lines as you usually do, changing nothing. Then sweep the final stroke firmly up, as in figure 137. Don't let it droop down as in figure 136 or allow the word to droop below the base line.

After you've done this for a few days, consciously practice being optimistic in real-life situations. Begin the exercise again and watch for changes in your natural writing.

**136.** *The finals in this sample are drooping down, showing sadness or depression.*

**137.**

## EXERCISE FOR FORWARD VISION

If self-castigation traits are appearing in your handwriting, it's necessary to counterbalance them. Do this exercise slowly. First, choose a word and fill up the page naturally, with your backward configuration. Try to *feel* the emotions that are bringing you back to the past. Then gradually and consciously bring the backward formation of the final stroke forward again, until you make it disappear entirely (Fig. 138).

138.

Optimism, enthusiasm, forward vision, and self-awareness are surefire ingredients in making successful changes and projecting yourself effectively. With the right attitude, you can learn to take charge and move ahead positively.

You should never think that you *have* to cope with an undesirable situation; there's always a way out. Obviously, some situations are more difficult than others, but I've never come across a case in which the person didn't have at least one option available. A simple change of environment, for instance, may be enough to alleviate pressure permanently or until other significant changes can be made.

The key to options counseling is in finding out who you are *now*. What suited you five years ago, or ten years ago, or six months ago may not be what suits you now. Handwriting analysis reflects the present, and that's what counts when you're assessing your needs or anyone else's.

In my options counseling practice I find out what traits work best for my clients—which is what I do in all phases of handwriting analysis. The things that work best for you are obviously the ones that will put you on a happy, fulfilling path. Everyone can utilize the abilities and talents they have; it's all a matter of positioning them correctly.

This case study is an example of how options counseling enabled a man dissatisfied with his life situation to make changes and project himself positively:

In his late thirties, married and the father of two older children, Edward Redmond found himself completely unhappy with his work and its effects on his home life. He was frequently tense, anxious, and stressed—feelings he unavoidably took out on his family.

At the age of thirty, Mr. Redmond had inherited the family business, a small company that manufactures electronic capacitors. As president of the firm, his duties entailed administrative functions of a maintenance nature; as a vendor for a standardized product, the post held little excitement for him.

I examined Mr. Redmond's handwriting (Fig. 139) and found that he had a gift for artistic communication and a

**139.** *Both upper and lower loops in Mr. Redmond's sample show creativity and imagination. Confusion about his affairs is also shown—the loops extend into the next line of writing.*

need to express himself creatively. In our counseling session Mr. Redmond revealed that he'd always wanted to be an artist. But as an only child, he also felt duty-bound to carry on the family business, so he pushed aside his real desires for what he felt he should do.

Bolstered by my analysis, Mr. Redmond was able to recognize his choices and work out a plan that suited both his and his family's needs. Opting to follow his original desire, Mr. Redmond decided to pursue a career as an illustrator. He knew he would have to start from scratch, but he was willing to make the effort this required.

He eventually enrolled in an art school in Chicago and began building his portfolio. Meanwhile, he maintained his interest in the company by hiring a new president suited to the job of management and by retaining his seat on the board of directors.

Although Mr. Redmond's interest in the family business still provided him with an adequate income, the reduction in pay caused by his leaving the presidency spurred his wife into considering re-entering the job market, a move she'd been contemplating for some months.

Together, the couple made a long-range plan to move within easy commuting distance of Chicago, where both Mr. Redmond and his wife would be able to pursue their respective careers.

Recognizing options and taking action, plus establishing short- and long-term goals, gave both Mr. and Mrs. Redmond a positive, new perspective. As a result, each was rejuvenated. Their lives flourished.

When clients come to me and they are at a crossroads, the first thing I tell them to do is to discover themselves. It's up to all of us who want to take charge of our lives to be aware of what we're all about. Your happiness depends on meeting your needs as they exist *now*.

Often, in the process of counseling clients, I not only give them the exercises that are in this book but suggest, as a potent means of getting to know themselves, that they keep a diary. You may want to try it, too.

The diary can take many forms. Generally, I suggest listings, such as: things that make me angry, things that please me, things I like to do best, things I resent doing, things I would like to be doing, and so on (Fig. 140). The results are usually incredibly illuminating, and people tell me they discover things about themselves that they weren't aware of before. You'll probably find it an eye-opener, too!

Not only is keeping the diary an exercise in self-awareness, but it's also a way of extending your vision to en-

Self-awareness Diary

Things that:

| Please me | Make me angry | I want to do | I do best |
|---|---|---|---|
| ice cream | waiting for buses | sail the South Pacific | make friends |
| English soccer matches | not getting some- where on time | make lots of money | play football |
| riding my bike with the wind behind me | incompetence | travel freely | give people advice |
| a cool coke on a hot day | missing the start of a movie | eat in the best restaurants | understand the needs of others |
| dogs & cats as pets | finding flaws in clothes when you get them home. | ride the Space Shuttle | carpentry |

140.

compass all kinds of possibilities. Being flexible, adaptable, aware, and open to every option will help you develop a positive, adventurous outlook. On the other hand, if you close yourself off to experience, you'll limit yourself tremendously.

Some people are naturally open, and others have to work at being open. The latter takes discipline. Here are some exercises I recommend for greater self-awareness, confidence, and discipline:

### EXERCISE FOR OPENING UP

This exercise is done on the familiar legal-size page. Again, fill up one or two sheets of paper. Choose a word that contains e's, a's, o's, or all three. Write that word, making sure these letters are full and round and contain no loops, as in figure 141. When you've done this for a few days, progress to a short sentence, making sure all the e's, a's, and o's are round and full.

During this exercise, I often suggest to my clients that they try things they've never done before. You might want to consider it, too. This could range from trying a new ethnic cuisine to taking a share in a group summer or ski house.

boater boater boater boater boater
boater boater boater boater boater

my boat floats everywhere. my boat
floats everywhere. my boat floats
everywhere. my boat floats everywhere

141.

Give yourself permission to fully experience your new situation. You may choose not to repeat it, but at least you've made a positive attempt to open yourself up.

## EXERCISE FOR EXPANSIVENESS

Fill up one or two pages of your legal pad with your signature. But for this exercise open it up; write it big and full and flowing (Fig. 142). You don't have to write this way all the time, but you should explore the feelings writing this way sparks.

142.

## EXERCISE FOR SELF-DISCIPLINE

Small handwriting indicates an ability to concentrate and exercise self-discipline. Let's face it, self-discipline isn't easy. Many people go to professionals to learn how to develop it. But this is an exercise you yourself can do effectively.

Start by writing a short sentence over and over again in your normal handwriting (Fig. 143). As you proceed down the page, gradually write smaller and smaller. On the last three days that you do this exercise, fill up the page with the tiniest writing you can manage. Try to *feel* the emotions of self-discipline.

This exercise won't change your handwriting, but it will give you the opportunity to feel a control you may not have experienced before without feeling anxious. You'll realize you can discipline yourself.

As you do this exercise you should relate it to your life. You have to practice self-discipline to make it work. If you have trouble with this, go back and do the exercise again.

Excuses and rationalizations aren't acceptable if you're not happy with what you're doing. If a client of mine says, "Yes, I agree I need a change, but I just can't do it," I recognize that that person lacks drive, and so I set him or her to work on drive exercises (those involving *t* bars on pages 138 and 140). The point is there are always options and you *can* take charge of them!

*I want to concentrate. I want to concentrate. I want to concentrate. I want to concentrate. I want to concentrate. I want to concentrate. I want to concentrate. I want to concentrate. I want to concentrate. I want to concentrate. I want to concentrate. I want to concentrate. I want to concentrate. I want to concentrate. I want to concentrate. I am concentrating. I am concentrating. I am concentrating. I am concentrating. I am concentrating. I am concentrating. I am concentrating. I am concentrating. I am concentrating. I am concentrating. I am concentrating. I am concentrating. I am concentrating. I am concentrating. I am concentrating. I am concentrating. I am concentrating. I am*

143.

## Graphotypes and the Way You Project Yourself

Your emotional responsiveness, your Graphotype, is one of the key characteristics through which you project yourself to the world. Your ability to sell yourself effectively is also linked to your Graphotype.

One of the major ingredients in the successful selling of your personality and in establishing good relationships is your ability to empathize—to understand someone else's feelings and point of view. This ability to empathize is found in the Graphotype.

All Plus-area Graphotypes have the ability to empathize to some degree. But obviously, not all Plus Graphotypes are going to be able to project themselves optimally or sell themselves most efficiently. This is where a close scrutiny of the other traits comes in.

For example, Supratypes are not overtly emotional, but when they have positive traits they can empathize well. Add reductive traits such as resentment, repression, or conservatism, though, and the Supratype's ability to understand the feelings and needs of others is severely limited (Fig. 144).

Another example of how someone can thwart his or her own sales ability is seen in the Extrotype who cuts off his or her innate capacity to empathize. Extrotypes are naturally warm and outgoing, but traits such as irritability, resentment, or temper can make them too impulsive or negatively emotional to project themselves effectively (Fig. 145).

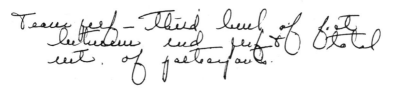

**144.** *Sensitivity to criticism (pronounced t and d loops) is so apparent that this Supratype's ability to project is diminished.*

As I've mentioned already, Introtypes have trouble reaching out, so their withdrawal and lack of empathy greatly reduce their ability to sell themselves effectively and project themselves to the world.

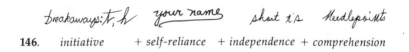

**145.** *This Extrotype shows too much confusion of interests to be projecting effectively.*

### The Evaluation Process

I've given you many individual traits so far and shown you how traits work in relation to one another. I'm going to end this chapter with specific examples of how certain traits in combination are indicative of other characteristics of personality.

The following examples are traits that are helpful in selling yourself and projecting a positive image to the world.

**146.**    *initiative*    + *self-reliance*   + *independence* + *comprehension*

The person with *daring* has the traits of initiative, self-reliance, independence, and comprehension.

*Tall Ts*    *t bar high*    *flourishes*

147.   vanity          + high goals        + showmanship

The individual who is *impressive* has some vanity, high goal placement, and showmanship.

*breakaway: t*   *v formation: m, n h*   *buckle very large*

148.   initiative       + analytical ability      + defiance

The *resourceful* person shows initiative, analytical ability, and a touch of defiance.

*Needlepoints*   *good lower loops*   *vis: m, n, h's*   *double loops*

149. comprehension    + imagination    + analytical ability    + deceit

The *shrewd* individual has good comprehension, imagination, analytical ability, and a bit of deceit.

*formations slope up*   *sweeping t bar*   *light pressure*

150.    optimism          + enthusiasm         + light pressure

*Resilience* is present when the individual has a combination of optimism, enthusiasm, and light pressure.

*forward slant*   *sweeping t*   *long, heavy t bar*

151.    Plus Graphotype    + enthusiasm     + willpower

*Dynamic* individuals are Plus Graphotypes with enthusiasm, willpower, and no indications of timidity or inhibitions.

*lower loop breakaway*          *long straight lower loop*

*breakaway: t*   + aggression   *long, heavy t bar* + determination   *optimism*

152. initiative        + willpower                    + positive outlook

The *forceful* person has initiative, aggression, willpower, determination, and a positive outlook.

*breakaway:* ⁄          *high T bars + initial hooks*

**153.**    *initiative*                          *+ ambition*

*Enterprising* types show initiative coupled with ambition.

*long finals*          *large I loops*          *soft strokes*

**154.**    *generosity*          *+ responsibility*          *+ yieldingness*

*Accommodating* individuals are those who have the traits of generosity, responsibility, yieldingness, and no indication of resentment or selfishness.

*breakaway:* ⁄          *lower loop breakaway*          *long. heavy t bar*

**155.**    *initiative*          *+ aggressiveness*          *+ willpower*

*tie strokes*          *long straight lower loop*          *optimism*

*+ persistence*          *+ determination*          *+ positive outlook*

The *go-getter* shows initiative, aggressiveness, willpower, persistence, determination, and a positive outlook.

*umbrella t bar*    *tapering m's*    *long finals*    *clear, wide e*

**156.** *self-control + diplomacy*          *+ generosity*          *+ broad-mindedness*

The person who is *patient* has self-control, diplomacy, generosity, and broad-mindedness, with no indications of irritability or temper.

*round i dot*          *clear circle letters*          *tie strokes*

**157.**    *loyalty*          *+ frankness*          *+ persistence*

The *conscientious* person shows loyalty, frankness, and persistence, without indications of deceit.

# 5 The Business World and Your Career

During the 1970s the business community found out what many individuals had known right along—that handwriting analysis is a very effective process. So graphology, long used in Europe, emerged as one of the most important and essential personality assessment methods available to American industry.

As of this writing, more than three thousand U.S. companies now employ staff or consultant graphologists in their personnel departments and use them on a regular basis. Their functions include screening job applicants, evaluating candidates for promotion and relocation, executive development, colleague compatibility studies, partnership arrangements, mergers and acquisitions, and outplacement —in short, any area dealing with people.

All types of businesses avail themselves of handwriting analysis—manufacturing firms, financial houses, service organizations, marketing corporations, government agencies, and law enforcement bureaus.

The implication of all this is that whether you're doing the hiring or being hired, handwriting analysis is more than likely to touch you in your career, especially as more companies awaken to its benefits. So you may not only be involved in graphology on the individual level (self-awareness, options counseling, vocational guidance, etcetera) but in the larger sense, too.

This chapter starts with the broad picture—how companies using graphology influence your career—and ends with how *you* can use handwriting analysis to help you in your choice of job and career.

### Personnel Screening

Currently, the greatest use of graphology in the business world is in screening job applicants. Matching the right person to the right job is a major part of my business at A New Slant, Inc.

My own method of evaluating job applicants involves the examination of approximately three hundred traits of personality, which takes from two to four hours to complete. The resultant information, which is kept confidential, gives me a complete portrait of the applicant's personality and all the information I need to see if he or she is right for the job.

Generally, personnel departments will make no effort to conceal from you the fact that they are using handwriting analysis as a testing method (Fig. 158). There's really no reason not to let you know, and I recommend to my corporate clients that applicants be made aware of it.

Handwriting analysis can be used at every level of hiring, from low-paying to high-paying jobs, from nonskilled to highly skilled, and from clerical to middle and top management posts. And that's the way it should be because, ultimately, people on all levels should be happy with what they're doing.

Corporation

Pre-Employment Graphoanalysis

Name _Bob R. R_

Date _March 11, 1980_

This form is provided for the purpose of obtaining a handwriting sample for graphoanalysis. It will not be decisive in whether or not you are hired by      Corporation, but will be used as a part of our over-all assessment of you as a potential employee.

INSTRUCTIONS: Using a ball-point pen or fountain pen ( no pencils or felt-tips, please) write on any subject of your choice. Write a passage long enough to fill the balance of this page.

HANDWRITING SAMPLE:

Bob R      is a very unique individual, and very sincere. At the age of 34, he left a secure position, successful in the American dream of a nice home, two cars, and a boat to return to college. He did this because he felt he had been second best for too long, and had become an underachiever, and he wanted to be recognized as a responsible, intelligent, and disciplined man. During his university experience, he was able to prove some things to himself, and now is ready to begin anew.

**158.** *This personnel form lets the applicant know handwriting analysis is being used as an evaluation method.*

A typical example of the effectiveness of personnel screening when handwriting analysis is used is shown here:

The president of a small market research firm was recently in search of a secretary. One woman was highly recommended by the personnel department on the basis of her interview and typing skills test, but the president wanted me to double check. When I received the sample I found many fine traits, but also saw that she wasn't suited to sitting behind a desk from nine to five (Fig. 159). I felt she would become resentful about being confined to a desk job, so based on my recommendation the woman wasn't hired for the job. I referred her to another department where she would be able to use her skills more effectively.

**159.** *The secretary's writing shows a need for movement and activity, which would not suit her to a typing job.*

Although this applicant seemed to be a very skilled and qualified secretary, the standard method of personnel screening apparently didn't get beyond her skills to consider her personality. In all probability, this woman wasn't happy with her work. Unfortunately, there are all too many people working at jobs that don't suit them. They may not realize there are other options for them. So they accept the work they have fallen into and either wait for something else to come along or plod on in unfulfilling jobs, collecting paycheck after paycheck, until retirement releases them from the drudgery of work that never really satisfied them. This scenario is sad but common—all the more reason to benefit from the knowledge available to you from graphology.

Just as graphology can help a company screen out an unsuitable job applicant, so it can work for an individual in the opposite way:

I was asked to review the writing of three people who applied for a paralegal position at a well-known law firm. The firm specialized in tax matters and I saw immediately that one applicant particularly excelled in analytical skills, mathematical aptitude, and ability to work with details (Fig. 160). I recommended this applicant because his skills and personality best suited the job. Based on my report, he was hired. Later, in a follow-up with the personnel department, I learned he had been the least favored of the three.

At his interview he appeared somewhat shy and dressed in a manner that, while neat, was considered dowdy. His references were impeccable, but he didn't make a good impression on his interviewer. What people often refer to as "chemistry" was lacking.

The favored applicants also had good references, but they were outgoing and dressed well. Their "chemistry" was acceptable. Yet chemistry is nothing more than a bias, and it was really the first applicant who was right for the job. Once he was in place he flourished and the firm was delighted with its choice.

In this case, if it wasn't for handwriting analysis, the best person for the job would have been passed over. One of the other two applicants may have worked out well enough, and the first probably would have gotten another job, but the

*of the conviction that "handwriting is brain writing" and that graphoanalysis of job seekers and/or agencies seeking a particular personality can be a decisive instrument that brings satisfaction to all concerned.*

*I would appreciate it if you would send me a sample of the check list you use for salespeople.*

*I am interested in the job as paralegal. I have had experience in this field and feel I could do a*

**160.** Top and middle: *These applicants were qualified for the job.*
Bottom: *But it was this person who got it. The small writing, showing ability to concentrate; retraced* p, *indicating precision; and analytical ability,* V *formations in the* n's *and* h's, *suited him well for the position.*

opportunity for a perfect union of the right person and the right job would have been lost. The law firm wouldn't be getting the best it could get and the applicant would have settled for something possibly less satisfying.

One of the best examples of job mismatching that I've seen is the case of former Secretary of State Alexander Haig. Haig's personality suited him well for the military but was all wrong for a career in diplomacy (Fig. 161). His handwriting shows that he has a brilliant analytic mind, with great vision and insight, but he lacks the trait of diplomacy (Fig. 162). Furthermore, it shows that he's very emotional and impetuous. His tendency to shoot from the hip is well documented—eventually it caused his resignation.

Haig's lot was made much worse by his incompatibility with his boss, President Ronald Reagan. Reagan's slightly backward slant (Fig. 163) shows emotions that are always under control. As an Introtype, Reagan lacks the empathy required to understand and tolerate Extrotype Haig's impulsive, emotional style.

**161.** *The strong handwriting of Alexander Haig shows impulsiveness but lacks diplomacy.*

**162.** *The trait for diplomacy is shown in tapering finals, especially in* m's *and* n's.

"You & I have a rendezvous with destiny. We can preserve for our children this, the last best hope of man on earth, or we can sentence them to take the first step into a thousand years of darkness. If we fail, at least let our children & our children's children say of us that we justified our brief moment here. We did all that could be done."

Ronald Reagan

**163**. *Ronald Reagan's slight backhand shows his emotions are under control.*

Another important benefit of handwriting analysis for personnel screening is in weeding out generally undesirable employees at the outset. In an age of mounting crime, especially in the white-collar area, it's tremendously important that dishonest individuals never get a chance to infiltrate organizations.

When I do an analysis for a company, I'm on the lookout for undesirable traits that show questionable behavior, such as:

**164.** Prejudice  *compressed letters, especially a's, o's, e's*
*intensified by: clannishness:* y g

**165.** Deceit  *double loops*

**166.** Superficial thinking  *no wedges or v's in m's, n's*
*or ill-formed m's, n's*

**167.** Withdrawal  *backward slant*

**168.** Shallowness  *concave t-bar*

**169.** Defiance  *big k buckle*

**170.** Selfishness  *compressed strokes + narrow e: e + initial hooks*

**171.** Exaggeration  *very large lower loops*

Obviously, one or two of these traits in a person's handwriting doesn't indicate a negative personality, especially if controls are developed. But certain combinations of traits or a preponderance of antisocial traits in a sample is a signal to steer clear of this job applicant. For example,

Many initial hooks + Many double loops =
Potentially dishonest

Here, the desire to acquire, plus the trait of deceit, could very well produce a thief, especially if other traits support it.

When the arrest of auto maker and entrepreneur John De-Lorean shocked the world, people couldn't believe that such a captain of industry allegedly was engaged in the shady practice of dealing in cocaine. Yet, in interviews given at the time, some people came forward and said that DeLorean had taken certain "offbeat" risks throughout his career. The public was further titillated by this news that a former top executive of General Motors had engaged in some business deals of apparently marginal integrity.

It's interesting to speculate on DeLorean's fate had hand-writing analysis been used to assess him at the outset of his career, or at any time when he made a major shift. Who knows where he'd be today.

Fortunately, most people are desirable workers who have good traits showing integrity. When I check for these traits I look for:

172. Ambition *high t bars + initial hooks*

173. Broad-mindedness *open e's, a's, o's*

174. Dignity *retraced t's, d stems*

175. Frankness *clean circle letters*

176. Loyalty *round i dot*

177. Pride *t's, d's 2-2½ times middle zone letters*

178. Sincerity *round i dot + no double loops*

179. Self-confidence *well-placed t bars + Large Capitals*

180. Self-control *convex t bar*

181. Independent thinking  *short t's, d's*

182. Generosity  *long finals*

If these traits are strong in your handwriting, you'll be a dedicated employee who puts the most into your job in order to get the most out of it.

When I'm asked to do a personnel screening, I look for problem areas, too. These are traits that have the potential to cause disruption in an employee's work routine and relationships with colleagues. Some of the more glaring are:

183. Argumentativeness  *p stem extends above*

184. Stubbornness  *Aent A (t)*

185. Arrogance  *vanity + backward slant + domineering: X*

186. Hysteria  *extreme right slant*

187. Irritability  *slashed i dot*

188. Hypercriticality
*investigative thinking: m, n* + *decisiveness: firm finals*
+ *large ego: I am* + *perfectionism: precise formations*
+ *narrowminded: closed i's, a's, o's*

189. Unrealistic imagination  *exaggerated lower loops*

190. Ultraconservatism  *very compressed letter formations*

191. Procrastination    *t bar on left only*

192. Sarcasm    *knife-like t bar*

193. Temper    *t bar on right only*

When I find these traits in a sample, I weigh them in the balance. For example, I look for control traits that compensate for the negative ones. And while the person may not be suitable for the job now, I like to give direction as to how he or she can improve for the future.

## Handwriting Analysis on the Job

Even after you've been hired, handwriting analysis can still work for you. It's a potent means of ensuring continued happiness and success in your job.

Promotions are one way in which handwriting analysis is used after hiring. A promotion is almost like applying for a new job. Generally your skills, dedication, and integrity are proven, but whether or not you can handle new or more responsibility is unknown.

In promotion evaluations, I look for traits that are likely to help a person handle a better job, such as:

194. Desire for responsibility    *large I and g loops*

195. Ability to handle pressure    *light writing retraced t,*

*d -* dignity    *M m, n m* · all thinking patterns

*t -* self-control    *vertical slant*
*t's, d's* -    pride

**196.** Attention to details     *well-placed i dots*

**197.** Organizational ability     *nicely formed, balanced f's*

If these are, in the main, lacking, I try to direct the individual to other options. Sometimes these traits are present, but there may be other problems, such as in this case:

The managing editor of a successful trade magazine was scheduled to retire within the year. Knowing this, the publisher, in agreement with the chief editor and retiring managing editor, chose a certain senior staff editor to fill the post.

But to the astonishment of his superiors, the man turned the promotion down. He was entreated again, and again he refused to accept. Yet his excellence as a journalist and his devotion and loyalty to the magazine were such that the publisher wouldn't take no for an answer. He asked me to examine the senior staffer's handwriting in the hopes of finding some way of convincing him to accept the promotion.

His managerial abilities were in evidence, but he couldn't handle stress and required a good deal of support in managing his work load (Fig. 198). Based on my advice, the publisher promised the senior man an editorial assistant. With this assurance, he was only too happy to accept the promotion.

When people are having problems on the job, handwriting analysis can be essential in helping both employee and employer. In a recent case I counseled, a computer programmer was on the verge of being fired. She'd proven herself in five years with the company, but over the last six months or so, her work had slipped significantly.

*I think it best to sum up this gathering tonight in the words of Sir Winston Churchill, who so eloquently put it, "Never before in the course of history have so many been asked to give so much for so little."*

**198**. *Heavy pressure and inattention to detail are two reasons why this senior editor didn't want the stress of a promotion.*

To all outward appearances she was the same, but an examination of her handwriting showed extreme emotional unrest. I advised her supervisor to have a sympathetic talk with her. It was discovered that the woman was going through an extremely traumatic divorce, which was affecting her work. But because she was intensely private and ashamed of the breakup of her marriage, she kept it to herself (Fig. 199). As it turned out, the programmer was given a short medical leave and later she was able to return to work productively.

Relocation evaluations are another way that handwriting analysis is used on the job. When a company decides to shift an employee from one location to another, it's a major move, so naturally everyone wants to make sure it's going to work out well for all concerned.

Transfers, too, are almost like starting from scratch, and screening methods are perfect for matching the right person to the right location, especially if the transfer involves a promotion, as is often the case. What's also of paramount

*one can read my writing — so I go along with society's rules. I like stark rooms too, simple clothes.*

*theres no one problem, such as career, that I*

**199.** *Withdrawn (backward slant) and a loner (no loops on g's and y's) made it difficult for this woman to reach out during the trauma of her marriage breakup.*

importance is that the employee's spouse find the move satisfying as well (Fig. 200).

If it turns out that the spouse isn't compatible with the new location and has made the change reluctantly, both marriage and career will suffer for it. When I do this kind of evaluation I give equal importance to the spouse, looking for his or her potentials and strengths. Recommendations based on this information are included in my report.

A relocation evaluation needn't be confined to long distances. The importance of any location or environment in relation to your happiness and productivity can't be underestimated. Here's a case study of a move made without the benefit of handwriting analysis:

Several years ago, the top management of a very successful newspaper decided to move the publication from an old building in the center of a small city to a new office complex in the suburbs. The move was anticipated by all with great enthusiasm, and eventually the entire staff was settled in its new location.

*I have worked for The*
*P.T.A for many weeks and*

**200.** *The large buckle in the k, showing defiance, and the tentlike t bar, showing stubbornness, add up to inflexibility in this person's writing. Also sensitive to criticism (inflated d loops), she found her husband's relocation from Virginia to Ohio difficult to accept.*

But it wasn't long before production and morale in the editorial department fell drastically. The once-happy editorial staff was disturbed by strife that hadn't existed before, especially among a group that was known for its stability. Many old-timers began looking for work elsewhere, and since the move, management has never been able to boost editorial morale or keep turnover under control.

Why such a drastic change? The planners of the new space didn't keep the needs of the editorial staff in mind.

In the old location the department was set up in the "bullpen" fashion—an entire floor with partitioned cubicles for editors and open spaces for the clerical and support staff. Communication among everyone flowed freely, and the air was brimming with the excitement of news stories coming in and being written.

In the new office building, modular construction and prefabricated wall elements made it possible to give each journalist a private office; each editor was placed in a small "cell," which opened onto a long corridor. There were few open spaces, and many of the offices had no windows. Communication was cut off and the general camaraderie and exchange enjoyed by the staff was lost for good. The planners had no concept of the relation of environment to personality, and so the new location was totally inappropriate to the type of work being conducted in it.

Had the services of a handwriting analyst been engaged, this travesty would never have happened. The environment would have been planned with the needs of the editorial staff in mind, and today the newspaper would still be enjoying staff stability, high morale, and excellent productivity.

On management levels, executives are using graphology to help them get ahead and remain productive in various ways. These include preparation for dealing with business people from other countries and backgrounds; negotiations, such as mergers and acquisitions; and strategic planning. In all of these cases it's important to know and understand the motivations and needs of those you're working with. Often management situations involve dealing with an "opponent." Obviously, if you can get a sample of his or her writing, you'll have an advantage in your negotiations. If you're in an opponent situation, look for:

201. Bluff *Exaggerated blunt downstrokes*

202. Aggression *lower loop breakaway strokes*

203. Yieldingness *"soft" rounded formations*

204. Deceit *double loops*

205. Frankness *clean circle letters*

206. Independent thinking *short t's and d's*

207. Decisiveness *long firm downstrokes*

208. Vanity *very tall t's*

209. Secretiveness *loop on right only*

**210.** Sincerity *round i dot + direct:*

*no initial strokes + frank: clear*

*circle letters*

**211.** Withdrawal *backward slant*

**212.** Directness *no initial strokes*

## Outplacement Evaluation

Outplacement is a relatively new area of business services. Outplacement departments of corporations or separate outplacement counseling agencies exist strictly to help terminated employees adjust to being fired. Although these services can deal with any strata of personnel, they're generally geared to management levels. Many outplacement facilities have handwriting analysts on staff or on retainer. The function of the outplacement department or agency is not to find jobs for people who have been fired but to help them cope and evaluate their present needs in terms of re-entry. At A New Slant, Inc., much of my work is involved with outplacement and essentially involves options counseling.

## Options Counseling and Your Career

In the section on options counseling in the preceding chapter, I've given you the insight you need to take charge of your life and make choices work for you in any situation.

Career-wise, however, there are a few more things you should know about your options. First of all, skills have little to do with your suitability for a job. That's why I've emphasized personality all along in this book. Skills are important in your job, of course, but in point of fact, statistics show that 85 percent of all job failures are related to personality factors; they're not skill oriented.

If you lack the right skills for the job, you'll find that out soon enough. But if your personality doesn't work, it's not so obvious to others—and perhaps not even to you. People are often unhappy with their work without knowing why.

It's worth making changes, as I've discussed. There are many options available, such as:

- Making a lateral move within a field or in the company
- Making a lateral move to another field or company
- Seeking more responsibility in a new post—accepting a challenge—within the present structure or on the outside
- Eliminating something from the existing job description
- Changing the environment without necessarily changing jobs or careers
- Changing careers, even if it entails retraining
- Finding an outside interest to eliminate or siphon off pressure

Often, people agree that they need to make a change but feel pressured to stay in a job they don't like because of the money they're earning. Sometimes it *is* impossible to change your career or job because of the practicality of earning a salary. But there are always options.

Instead, you could develop a hobby based on strong traits in your personality profile. Or you could teach or take a course at the local YWCA/YMCA or a similar institution. The point is, in both instances, to find a creative outlet for your career frustrations outside the job, developing strong traits and interests as an avocation.

## Women and Careers

Women are entering the work force in ever increasing numbers, especially in management positions. As a result, the roles of women (and men) in society are changing. For you, the working woman, this means striving toward equality in the labor market, as in the other areas of your life. It also means availing yourself of options counseling for optimal career planning.

Yet, as a woman, you're still regarded by many primarily as a homemaker, even when you're working, and no matter how much your spouse may contribute to maintaining the household. These dual roles can place many demands on you. Often, as a result, a woman must strive very hard to get ahead, so it's especially important to develop strong traits in your handwriting, such as determination, aggression, independence, and self-confidence.

Of the 40 million women in the U.S. work force—about 45 percent of the total work world—68 percent are working to support themselves. About 70 percent of all working women are still employed in the traditionally female-dominated areas: bookkeepers, waitresses, clericals, domestics, and elementary school teachers. Only 6 percent of working women are in managerial or administrative positions.

This last figure is changing. More women are seeking to hold better jobs that were once male dominated. As women become managers, they're developing traits of leadership such as ambition, well-placed goals, and persistence. Women are discovering their options and are moving beyond the old stereotypes. (See figures 213, 214.)

As a woman, discovering your options can help you realize that now, more than ever, many paths are open to you. You're realizing you can do exactly what suits you.

Accepting responsibility and change isn't always easy, though. All too often I see confusion in women's handwriting. This can stem from several things. Confusion can result when a woman is looking for a job and is torn between career paths or between remaining a homemaker and entering the work force (Fig. 215).

*We the people of the United States, in order to form a more perfect union, establish justice, insure domestic tranquility, & provide for the common defense, promote the general welfare, and secure the blessings of liberty to ourselves and our posterity . . .*

*Bella Abzug*

**213.** *Former Congresswoman Bella Abzug's strong writing shows the qualities that have made her a successful politician and businesswoman. These include strong thinking patterns, open-mindedness, enthusiasm, and self-confidence.*

It can also happen when a woman has too many irons in the fire. Often a working woman is pressured into believing she has to produce twice as much as a man to be valued. Too much is happening at once. In these cases, I recommend discipline exercises. I also recommend that, if possible, help be obtained to siphon off some of the work and the pres-

I get rid
of flabby
stomachs &
round shoulders

---

The Focus is what
is important I know
if we keep our eyes
on our goals we will
make it

Dear Shiela,

Please excuse my delay. Here is the xerox copy of the sample. M.

to prepare the analisis 13.
my future business ventu
and whether or not my
personality changes signifi

**214.** Facing page and above: *These samples were all written by very successful women in business. Can you spot the traits that helped make them successes?*

sure. In any event, this person should learn to tackle one thing at a time.

Fortunately, women are becoming more certain about what they really want to do and are learning to be true to themselves, no matter what their current position. This may include:

- A successful businesswoman ready to make a change
- A woman who wants to upgrade her current position
- A woman re-entering the job market
- A woman who has never worked before
- A woman who has done volunteer work before and who wants to enter a paying situation
- Or the woman who wants to move from a paying job into a volunteer situation

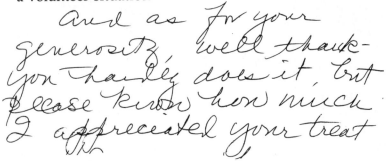

**215.** *Confusion, seen in the extension of lower loops into the next line of writing, is seen in this working woman's handwriting.*

In all of these instances the goal is the same: to find the career that suits you totally and makes your daytime hours work. It's been my experience in counseling women that when daytime hours are satisfying, every area of life flourishes.

Of course, not all women necessarily want to be (or can be) top managers. This case study shows just that:

A very successful businesswoman who worked her way up the corporate ladder in a pharmaceutical firm came to me

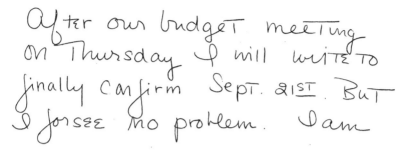

After our budget meeting on Thursday I will write to finally confirm Sept. 21ST. But I forsee no problem. I am

**216.** *Lack of follow-through (g's and y's do not return to base line) is one reason this woman executive found it hard to do what she really wanted.*

for counseling regarding a job change. Although settled in a financially rewarding executive post, she'd been dissatisfied with her work for some time (Fig. 216).

Her writing revealed that she wasn't good at handling stress or responsibility. In our counseling session, she told me her ambition since childhood was to be a nursery school teacher—she loved working with small children.

But she came from a background of wealth and status. Her grandmother had been a suffragette and her own mother was an attorney. This woman allowed herself to be manipulated into a profesional position she didn't really want because she was afraid of what her friends and family would say. Even with counseling she couldn't bring herself to do what she honestly wanted. She agreed to consider volunteer work with children as an outlet but wasn't sure the pressures of her job would permit it.

Unfortunately, this woman refused to recognize her options, all the more sad because money wasn't an issue. Her self-esteem was low and she couldn't get out of the trap of letting unrealistic values color her judgment.

This is an unusual case, but it nonetheless underscores the fact that no matter who or what you are, you have the power to make your own choices. A majority of women now want more responsibility and want to enter better jobs, which allow them to express themselves more fully. But no matter what your choice, of the hundreds of women I've counseled at A New Slant, Inc., the ones who succeed are those who are self-confident, optimistic, forward looking, and aware they have options. These traits are clearly evidenced in their handwriting. Successful women also realize they must get rid of the concepts of the past in order to do what's right for them.

The character-building exercises given throughout this book are ideal for women who face the task of getting beyond the old ways of thinking. In addition, the following exercise is designed to promote clarity of thinking, since, unfortunately, women who want to succeed are often nagged by doubts and past conditioning.

### EXERCISE FOR MENTAL CLARITY

Confusion is characterized by two signs in handwriting: both lower and upper loops consistently highly inflated (Fig. 217); and the downstrokes and lower loops of letters running into the words or sentences on the next line of writing (Fig. 218). In this exercise, we will deal with the latter.

On your legal pad, choose one or two sentences and fill up the page with them. As you move down the page, make sure that no downstroke touches the line of writing below.

Detangle both your writing and your life at the same time. Make a conscious effort to take things one at a time. How relieved you'll feel in just a month!

As a woman, your task is to realize that you don't have to become like a man to find fulfillment in your career. You can still be a woman and get all you want by being positively motivated and by taking advantage of all the options open to you.

upper loops inflated and running into
the writing above it and lower loops
inflated and running into the lines
below it.

217.

I'll try to sort things out. I'll try
to sort things out. I'll try to sort
things out. I'll try to sort things
out. I'll try to sort things out.
I'll try to sort things out. I'll try

218.

## Stress and Your Career

Are you exhausted after a routine day's work? Do you
need a drink to relax or do you just feel like flopping in bed?
If so, you, like so many others, are probably suffering from
stress. Stress, in varying degrees from worry to burnout,
affects many people in their careers. As a result, the field of
stress management is rapidly growing as more and more
people realize they need a way to handle their tensions and
anxieties.

Handwriting analysis is a potent stress management tool
in its own right because it shows you how much stress you
can take and helps you to discover what specific factors in
your personality affect it. For example, if your writing
shows an inability to handle responsibility, this may cause
stress, especially if you write with heavy pressure.

Worry is a factor in stress and is seen in the writing in inverted loops, especially in *m*'s and *n*'s (Fig. 219). If the person has other reductive traits, such as yieldingness (indecisive endings), jealousy (small loops in *m*'s and *n*'s), repression (retracing), and low self-esteem (low *t* bars), worry can turn from feelings of uneasiness to stress.

Often, we'll casually say that stress is caused by some kind of behavior, but really it's the *failure* to manage self-defeating behavior that causes stress. So, stress can be caused by problems such as:

- An inability to manage time properly
- An inability to make decisions
- Unrecognized role conflicts
- Procrastination
- Authoritarianism
- Perfectionism
- Fear of taking action

The surface reasons that appear to cause stress may be any one of the following:

- Need to stay at the top (ambition)
- A promotion that brings more responsibility
- Increased work load
- Personality conflicts with co-workers
- Responsibility for decision making
- Deadline pressure
- Strife in personal life

One way of pinpointing the exact causes of stress in your job (or life, for that matter) is to keep a diary. When you feel stress, write down the cause. You'll soon have a pretty clear idea of what adversely affects you.

If stress is unchecked, its effects can be very serious. Obviously, your body suffers. Emotionally, the entire quality of your life is diminished. In your career, untreated stress can inhibit creative problem solving and even block your abilities to use your skills effectively.

**219**. *Worry is seen in inverted loops, especially in* m's *and* n's.

If you're a manager, it's important to be alert to signs of stress not only in your own performance but also in the lives of people under you. You should know who in your department can and can't handle stress and assign work loads and responsibilities accordingly. If you know a worker can't handle stress but is otherwise very proficient, you can make allowances to deal with particularly stressful situations. The following case study is an example:

Once a year, the editorial staff of a trade magazine puts out an additional, special issue. This creates extra work for everyone but especially for the art director, who must coordinate everything (Fig. 220). The magazine's chief editor knows this man can manage only a certain amount of stress, so for those few weeks a year he hires a free-lance artist. Without the extra pressure, the art director is happy, and the entire magazine's staff benefits.

It would be easy for the chief editor to simply ignore the problem or to put up with a harried art director for a while, but instead he realizes that the few extra dollars he spends is worth the expense.

*The ad will be going in The March issue of the magazine — please have the graphics to*

**220.** *Inability to handle details well (slashed* i *dots) and the heavy pressure of the writing make it difficult for this art director to handle pressure.*

Understanding the stress levels of people who work together is important in putting together a team. The work load can be balanced in terms of who can and who can't handle stress so you won't wind up with a team of people, for example, in which no one handles stress well.

Stress can't and shouldn't be *totally* avoided. Mild stress is a positive and potent way to spur your performance. The trick is to learn how to handle stress and to train yourself not to let it undermine you.

When stress becomes so bad that burnout levels are reached, I recommend a complete change of profession rather than working within the framework of the existing one. I often direct teachers, for example, to move from the classroom into private industry, where they can still use their skills and knowledge. (See figure 221.)

You can learn to handle stress in a variety of ways. First, though, you must realize that stress doesn't come from career or business problems themselves but from the way you manage your feelings and attitudes toward them.

Look at the way you've handled stress in the past. If these methods were successful, use them again. If they weren't effective, you should work on developing new ways by

*In so many words, he communicated to me that I did not have the mental*

**221.** *This teacher has reached the burnout level. The sample shows much resentment, indicated by the inflexible approach strokes that start from the base line and lean against the letters.*

using your handwriting. Check for traits that block your ability to handle stress. Do you see irritability, for example? Or lack of follow-through? Or resentment? If so, practice all the exercises in *Graphotypes*, particularly the exercise for determination (page 78), the exercises for positive attitude (page 82), and the exercise for persistence (page 139).

Look to your good traits to help you develop controls. (You should develop controls rather than try to change the pressure you write with, which could be emotionally upsetting or traumatic. The complex characteristics underlying pressure are so interwoven with your entire temperament that you should work with a graphologist if you want to change them.) For example, if you have analytical or investigative ability, use it to get to the root of what's causing you stress. A sense of humor can help you handle stress, as can traits such as determination, organization, patience, and so on.

You can also eliminate a great deal of stress by realizing that you don't have to be something you aren't and that you don't have to do something that's not appropriate for you. Again, one of the cardinal rules of successful living through graphology is knowing yourself. So by overcoming your weak traits and utilizing your strong points you can work on stress.

For example, if you are sensitive to criticism (Fig. 222), avoid situations that invite criticism, and therefore stress until you are better able to deal with it. If you have a desire for physical activity (Fig. 223), athletics can be your outlet.

All of the exercises given in this book are useful in stress management. Here's an exercise that involves working with details. It's given to show you how you can overcome problems that cause stress.

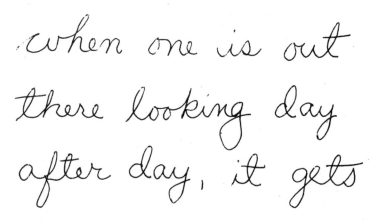

**222**. *Sensitivity to criticism is seen in the inflated* t *and* d *loops.*

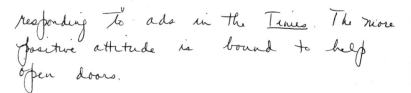

**223**. *This individual needs physical activity as seen in the inflated* p *loops.*


## EXERCISE FOR DETAIL ORIENTATION

The trait for dealing with detail is seen in the *i* dot. Choose a short sentence with many *i*'s in it. For the first two days, write it your own way a few times and then gradually begin dotting the *i*'s as close as possible to the stem (Fig. 224). For the remainder of the exercise, dot the *i* as close to the stem as you can. Think intensely about what you've done and how you feel. If you were extremely irritable, wait a few days before doing the exercise again.

OLD { *Write this initially in script. Write this in-*
*itially in script. Write this initially in script.*

NEW: *Write this initially in script. Write this*
*initially in script. Write this initially*
*in script. Write this initially in script.*
*Write this initially in script. Write this in-*
*itially in script. Write this initially in*
*script. Write this initially in script. Write*

**224.**

When stress is managed properly, you use both your skills and personality traits to the best advantage. You're more likely to have a good energy level, be flexible, and respond to change and variety (Fig. 225). Moreover, you'll be resilient and look forward to each day with gusto.

*Glad to hear the article*
*has worked out so well for you.*

**225.** *The need for change and variety is seen in the long, broad lower y loop.*

## Alcoholism

One of the extreme results of unmanaged stress is alcoholism. Unfortunately, I've seen too many cases of career-related alcoholism show up in handwriting samples, particularly among executives.

There's no consistent universal pattern of traits in a sample that definitely shows alcoholism. But graphological researchers have found that a preponderance of the samples of alcoholics do have backward capital *I*'s and distorted *J*'s. Other traits that are seen more frequently in the writing of alcoholics, as compared to the general public, are:

**226.** Sensuality

**227.** Guilt

**228.** Temper

**229.** Resentment

**230.** Sensitivity to criticism

**231.** Low goal orientation

**232.** Sarcasm

**233.** Confusion of interests

**234.** Depression

**235.** Desire for attention

**236.** Yieldingness

Writing done under the influence of alcohol markedly shows the undesirable traits and physiological deterioration brought on by drinking (Fig. 237). Alcoholics lose their inhibitions, and this also shows in their writing: some writings show extreme hostility or aggressiveness, for example, and others may show deception or lying.

*sorry I wasn't available to come to the meeting yesterday. Unfortunately I was tied up and couldn't get to*

**237.** *This alcoholic's handwriting shows corrugations and some muddiness, as well as fairly low goals.*

Handwriting analysis is useful in detecting and treating alcoholism in that it (1) calls attention to the problem, (2) permits the graphologist to suggest that the person get help, and (3) monitors changes when the individual is under treatment.

Treatment of alcoholism, be it via Alcoholics Anonymous, psychiatry, or some other means is based on the alcoholic's taking personal responsibility for total abstinence. Therefore, a key to recovery is in encouraging the person to become motivated and establish goals.

Finding the strengths in an alcoholic's handwriting can help the person choose a new view of life, build self-confidence, think creatively, and communicate (Fig. 238). This, in conjunction with a supervised treatment program, can go a long way in helping an alcoholic recover.

## Other Addictions

Alcoholism isn't the only addiction that can result from unmanaged stress. Others can include, for example, excessive cigarette smoking, drug use, overeating, and gambling.

Research has shown that addictive individuals are basically self-destructive and compulsive. A new study, conducted by Alan Lang, professor of psychology at Florida State University, concludes that no single set of psychological characteristics exists that embrace all addictions. However, the report states that "significant personality factors" can contribute to addictive personalities. These are:

- Impulsive behavior
- Difficulty in delaying gratification
- Sensation seeking
- Antisocial personality
- A high value placed on nonconformity
- Weak commitment to goals
- A tolerance for deviation
- A sense of alienation

*Thought you'd like to have the enclosed.*

**238**. *This recovered alcoholic has practical goals and is working to maintain his rehabilitation as seen by the umbrellalike t bar on the capital, the trait for self-control.*

## The Evaluation Process

Some of the interactive traits needed for success in business and career are described below. Notice how each trait contributes to the makeup of the characteristic described.

*t bar crossed middle*     *wedges: M*  *v forms: m*    *compressed letters*

**239**. *practical goals + logical thinking patterns + conservatism*

The person who has *common sense* shows practical goals, logical thinking patterns, and conservatism.

*deep wedges: M*    *sweeping t bar*    *initial hooks*

**240**. *exploratory thinking patterns + enthusiasm + acquisitiveness*

One who is *eager to learn* has exploratory thinking patterns, enthusiasm, and acquisitiveness.

*soft strokes*    *lack of:*  *t form*    *lack of:*  *slashed i*

**241**. *yielding + no temper + no irritability*

The *agreeable* individual is yielding and shows no temper or irritability.

*round i dot*    *clear circle letters*    *clear, wide e's*

**242**. *loyalty + honesty (frankness) + open-mindedness*

The *faithful* person shows loyalty, honesty, and open-mindedness.

*vertical or backward slant*
*self-control*

$t$ *form*

**243.** *cool and poised*          + *no temper*

The *levelheaded* individual is cool, poised, and without temper.

*round i dot*   *tall t's, d's*   *tie strokes*   *long straight finals*

**244.** *loyalty*      + *pride*      + *persistence*      + *determination*

One who is *reliable* shows loyalty, pride, persistence, and determination. Deceit and confusion are absent.

*vertical or backward slant*
*caution*
*convex T bar*

*clear, wide e's*

**245.**      *poise*              + *broad-mindedness*

The *fair* person has no deceit but does show poise and broad-mindedness.

*tie strokes*      *well-dotted i's*

**246.**   *persistence*      + *detail orientation*

The *diligent* person has persistence and the ability to pay attention to details.

*needlepoints*

**247.** *comprehension*

*v form: m, n's  h's*

+ *analytical ability*

*breakaway:*

+ *initiative*

*breaks in letters*

+ *intuition*

People with *foresight* have good comprehension, initiative, analytical ability, and intuition.

*clear circle letters*

**248.** *honesty (frankness)*

*tie strokes*

+ *persistence*

*tall t's, d's*

+ *pride*

*long straight finals*

+ *determination*

*optimism*

+ *positive outlook*

*Dependable* people show honesty, pride, persistence, determination, and a positive outlook, with no deceit.

*well-dotted i's*

**249.** *detail orientation*

*retraced p*

+ *precision*

*tie strokes*

+ *persistence*

*long, straight finals*

+ *determination*

*final hooks*

+ *tenacity*

The *thorough* individual has detail orientation, precision, persistence, determination, and tenacity.

*Needlepoints*     *sweeping t-bar*     *tall t's, d's*

**250**. *comprehension*     + *enthusiasm*     + *pride*

*breakaway: t   high goals (t)*     *ē Large Capitals*

+ *initiative*     + *self-confidence*

*Leaders* have strong traits of comprehension, enthusiasm, pride, initiative, and self-confidence. Traits of timidity and self-doubt are lacking.

# 6 Your Vocational Guide

Choosing a profession is one of the most important decisions you'll ever make in your life. By now, you probably have a good idea of where your strengths and weaknesses lie. You know what your interests are. You may be happy in your career or you may want to move in another direction. Or you may be picking a vocation for the first time.

The information I've given you in *Graphotypes* will help you make choices with clarity and confidence. To give you further guidance, I've put together a vocational guide, which lists many careers and tells you what traits are needed for success in them. I know you'll find it helpful.

As an example, I'm also going to talk about one career at length in this chapter—sales—for two reasons. First, there are a lot of people who make it their vocation. Second, as I pointed out in Chapter 4, "Projecting Yourself to the World," every aspect of life involves selling. Even if your job isn't selling per se, many of the elements of the sales profession can be successfully incorporated in the career you choose.

## Sales as a Profession

If you want to pursue sales as a career, you should have or develop a sales personality. This means you should be able to sell anything, especially yourself. There are many elements that go into making you a successful salesperson. For one thing, you should have the ability to empathize, which is indicated in your emotional responsiveness, or Graphotype. Extrotypes and Supratype Plus individuals respond most empathetically. Supratypes are also able to empathize, but Introtypes generally lack this ability. Introtypes can succeed in sales, though, because they learn how to please people.

As a successful salesperson, you should also have ego drive and the need to conquer. The nature of selling is such that you'll probably encounter more failures than successes. You should be prepared for this and learn not to take the failures personally.

Ego drive is indicated by a well-formed large capital *I* (Fig. 251).

Feelings of rejection or disappointment are reflected when loops are made backward (Fig. 252).

Empathy and ego drive should be balanced for maximum effectiveness, otherwise your success is undermined. If you have empathy, for example, but lack ego drive, you may be unable to close the deal. This is not uncommon. I'm sure everyone knows of a salesperson who has a terrific personality but simply fails to get the sale. On the other hand, if you have drive but lack empathy, you may bulldoze your way through a sale. This tactic works sometimes, but in the long run, your lack of understanding will meet with more failures than successes.

**251**. *A well-formed large capital* I *indicates ego drive.*

**252.** *Backward loops indicate feelings of disappointment.*

Other characteristics that make up a successful salesperson are organizational ability, shown in the balance of the *f* loops, and the ability to be analytical, seen in V formations in *m*'s, *n*'s, and *h*'s.

If you want to excel in sales, I've devised a few exercises that will help you build your sales personality.

### EXERCISE TO IMPROVE EMPATHY

Exchange pen and paper with someone you know. Try to copy his or her handwriting as exactly as you can, emulating pressure and style. What you are doing is drawing someone else's personality. As you are doing this, allow yourself to experience your feelings. Voice them out loud or write them down. Exactly what do you feel—and are they *your* feelings or part of the personality of the other person? Do you feel new emotions? Is the exercise easy or difficult? Explore all these possibilities.

**253.** *Politicians must sell themselves to stay in office. Vice-President George Bush's handwriting shows a direct, analytical approach.*

**254.** *Leonard Bernstein's handwriting shows flair and showmanship, as well as an all-round sales personality.*

## EXERCISE TO BUILD ENTHUSIASM

Practice sweeping your *t* bars. Fill up a page of your pad with *t*'s bearing sweeping crosses. Do this for a few days. Then, progress to your signature (if your name has a *t* in it) or to a short sentence with a lot of *t*'s in it. Be sure you're sweeping the *t* bars as you progress (Fig. 255).

**255.**

## EXERCISE FOR PERSISTENCE

Your stick-to-it-iveness is based on your ability to persist. Without this trait you'll find it difficult to reach your goals. In this exercise, write a line of *t*'s crossed with tie strokes. Next, write a line of *f*'s with tie strokes. Fill up one piece of paper with these alternating lines of *f*'s and *t*'s (Fig. 256). In your daily routine, as you write, consciously write tie strokes in all the letters you can think of, not just *t*'s and *f*'s (Fig. 257). Look at your writing at the end of the day to see if you've left out too many possibilities for tie strokes.

**256.**

**257.** *Notice how tie strokes are incorporated throughout this sample.*

## EXERCISE FOR GOAL ORIENTATION

In the morning when you get up, set a goal to accomplish by the end of the day. The goal can be anything and needn't be complicated. Follow through by achieving your goal and by filling up one page with *t*'s crossed as near the top of the stem as is comfortable for you (Fig. 258).

258.

Sometimes, when a salesperson isn't working up to full potential, it could mean that a change is needed. As I've discussed in preceding chapters, options counseling is essential if you've come to such a crossroads.

**Your Sales Performance Profile**

The following checklist shows traits needed for an effective sales personality:

*Positive Sales Traits*

259.

Stamina
Vitality = Energy level = Heavy writing pressure

260. Empathy = Emotional responsiveness = Plus Graphotypes

261. Persistence *persistence*

262. Motivation (Goal orientation) *motivation*

263. Self-starter *high T bars + initiative ( ↑ ) + determination (y)*

264. Control of impulses *control*

265. Enthusiasm *enthusiastic*

266. Persuasion *talkative (open a's, c's) + persistent (+)*

267. Initiative *initiative ( ↑*

268. Self-reliance *my name*

269. Tenacity *tenacity*

270. Broad-mindedness *broadminded*

271. Imagination *imagination*

272. Intuition *intuition*

273. Diplomacy *diplomacy : m m*

274. Dignity *dignity*

275. Showmanship *Showmanship*

These traits can reduce the effectiveness of your sales:

*Negative Sales Traits*

276. Impatience    *slashed i*

277. Confusion of interests    *confusion of interests*

278. Sarcasm    *sarcastic*

279. Disorganization    *disorganization my friend*

280. Vanity    *vanity*

281. Lack of integrity    *heightened by: • shallowness: t*
   *double loops*    *• evasiveness: hook in circle letters*
   *• other reductive traits*

282. Inability to follow through    *no persistence or determination: g.y.j.*

283. Too much aggression    *breakaway strokes in lower loops everywhere*

284. Inability to listen    *too much talkativeness*

285. Procrastination    *procrastination*

286. Sensitivity to criticism    *sensitive to criticism*

**Your Vocational Trait Checklist**

Here is a list of careers in alphabetical order and the key traits needed to function successfully in each:

| *Career* | *Key Traits* |
|---|---|
| Accountant | Analytical ability, good aptitude for numbers and details, precision, concentration, sensitivity to criticism, patience, objectivity; Supratype or Introtype. |
| Air traffic controller | Sense of responsibility, quick thinking, concentration, ability to handle details and stress, stable emotions, not impulsive. |
| Architect | Rhythm, fluidity, imagination, intuition, ability to handle details, line and color appreciation. |
| Artist | Ability to visualize, color sense, line appreciation, patience, originality, manual dexterity, handles heavy pressure. |
| Athlete | Strong determination and persistence, stamina, courage, initiative, enthusiasm, pride, cooperation, precision. |
| Banker | Integrity, ability to handle details, mathematical ability, dignity, diplomacy, loyalty, pride, self-control. |
| Building contractor | Decisiveness, initiative, self-confidence, precision, rhythm, imagination, ability to handle details and numbers, organization. |
| Building trade | Manual dexterity, ability to handle details and solve number problems quickly, pride, initiative, stamina, rhythm. |

| | |
|---|---|
| Chef | Organization, ability to supervise and handle details, decisiveness, independent thinking, high energy level. |
| Clergy | Love of people, open-mindedness, loyalty, integrity, expressiveness, organization, pride, dignity, decisiveness, generosity, frankness. |
| Clerical career | Dependability, ability to handle details, organization, patience, good memory, ability to deal with people. |
| Computer programmer | Clear and logical thinking, analytical ability, patience, persistence, accuracy, abstract imagination, determination, tenacity, ability to work under pressure. |
| Cosmetologist | People orientation, patience, quick responses, precision, tact, ability to handle details, organization, open-mindedness, color appreciation, manual dexterity. |
| Credit official | Analytical ability, diplomacy, good judgment, people orientation, intuitiveness, decision-making ability, verbal and written skills; self-starter. |
| Dietician | Organization, administrative ability, scientific aptitude, ability to handle details, flexibility, patience, analytical ability. |
| Draftsman | Ability to handle details, manual dexterity, concentration, precision, artistic ability, originality, logical and careful thinking. |
| Educator | Open-mindedness, objectivity, analytical ability, high energy level, en- |

thusiasm, dignity, loyalty, people orientation, expressiveness—both verbally and written—integrity, ability to handle details.

Employment counselor Objectivity, clerical aptitude, ability to talk and listen, stamina, patience, determination, persistence, will-power, research ability, generosity, organization, enthusiasm, ability to handle details.

Engineer Stamina, leadership, precision, cautiousness, manual dexterity, pride, careful and methodical thinking, analytical ability, concentration, independence, scientific curiosity, integrity.

Farming professional Strong willpower, decisiveness, imagination, initiative, organization, emotional balance, physical stamina, directness, broad-mindedness.

Fashion designer Good color sense, artistic ability, imagination, rhythm, enthusiasm, stability, resourcefulness, self-confidence, pride, manual dexterity, determination, loyalty.

Forester Organization, ability to work alone, initiative, physical stamina, poise, investigative powers.

Government service Ability to take orders, follow-through, tolerance of routine, pride, dignity, loyalty, stamina, ability to handle details.

Graphologist Analytical ability, intuitiveness, investigative powers, people orientation, verbal and written expres-

| | |
|---|---|
| | sion, persistence, determination, organization, diplomacy, ability to handle details. |
| Hospital administrator | Initiative, organization, ability to handle details, patience, good speaking ability, diplomacy, analytical ability, determination, decisiveness, self-starter; Plus-area Graphotype. |
| Hotel/motel manager | Supervisory capabilities, clerical skills, initiative, self-discipline, organization, people orientation, stable emotions, decisiveness, free of hostility. |
| Independent business owner | Independence, initiative, clerical abilities, willpower, determination, persistence, organization, ability to handle details, good memory, pride, tolerance for routine, adaptability, open-mindedness. |
| Industrial designer | Creative talent, intuitiveness, empathy, drawing skills, persistence, sales ability, organization, initiative, color awareness. |
| Investment broker | Integrity, investigative powers, communication skills, ability to handle details and numbers, organization. |
| Legal profession | Integrity, leadership ability, high goals, writing skills, strong thinking patterns, dignity, calmness and composure, initiative, ability to handle details, patience. |
| Literary *Author:* | Literary ability, ability to work alone and handle details, analytical |

|  | and investigative ability, emotional depth, tolerance of routine, clarity of thought, ability to handle rejection. |
| --- | --- |
| *Journalist:* | Need for change and variety, literary talent, ability to work under pressure and handle details, initiative, people orientation, good energy. |
| *Librarian:* | Good memory, open-mindedness, patience, ability to work alone and handle details, organization. |
| Music field | Intuition, tenacity, manual dexterity, sense of rhythm, precision, determination, good memory, deep feelings, analytical ability, patience. |
| Oceanographer | Research ability, intellectual curiosity, patience, ability to work well with others, self-direction, determination, initiative, strong willpower, confidence, good communication skills. |
| Pharmacist | Ability to handle details, confidence, scientific aptitudes, exploratory and analytical abilities, caution, frankness, directness, integrity. |
| Photographer | Patience, manual dexterity, imagination and originality, quick thinking, responsiveness, persistence, artistic ability, color sense. |
| Physical welfare *Physician, surgeon, dentist, nurse, physical therapist* | Interest in people, integrity, manual dexterity, empathy, ability to handle details, tact, good memory, scientific aptitudes. |

| | |
|---|---|
| Police professionals | Investigative ability, determination, objectivity, good judgment, no impulsiveness, integrity, pride, open-mindedness, diplomacy, directness, frankness, organization, ability to deal with facts, stable emotions, generosity, warmth. |
| Printing | Ability to handle stress and details, organization, analytical ability, reliability. |
| Psychologist/ psychiatrist | Intuition, perception, analytical ability, good comprehension, integrity, diplomacy, ability to talk and listen and handle stress, patience. |
| Publishing | Investigative ability, patience, concentration, ability to handle details, fluidity, analytical and objective thinking, verbal skills, communications ability, diplomacy, intuition, ability to listen. |
| Radio/television announcer | Emotionally responsive, expressive, enthusiastic, sense of humor, self-confidence, diplomacy, dignity, rhythm, purpose, directness, frankness, determination, willpower, aggressiveness, imagination, perceptiveness. |
| Real estate broker | Honesty; maturity; ability to handle stress, numbers, and details; tact; enthusiasm; good memory; factual and imaginative thinking; initiative; decisiveness; optimism; analytical and investigative ability; ability to think and act independently. |

| | |
|---|---|
| Rehabilitation services | Emotional stability, empathy, ability to handle details and work independently, objectivity, patience, scientific aptitude, tact, imagination, sensitivity. |
| Sales | Enthusiasm, responsiveness, initiative, persistence, integrity, self-confidence, acquisitiveness, intuition, expressiveness, poise, dignity, open-mindedness, need for change and variety, quick thinking, loyalty, self-starter. |
| Social worker | Poise, objectivity, self-confidence, ability to handle details, diplomacy, open-mindedness, intuition, investigative ability, good judgment, enthusiasm. |
| Truck driver | Manual dexterity, practicality, willpower, determination, initiative, integrity, pride, ability to handle details. |
| Urban planner | Imagination, practicality, organization, tact, objectivity, directness, expressiveness, verbal and written skills, people orientation. |

# 7 Kid's Stuff: Handwriting of Children and Young Adults

Can any one of us look back on the penmanship classes of our youth with fondness? My guess is that few of us really enjoyed learning how to write script. For most, copying the letters on the chart until they were perfect was a torturous exercise.

Penmanship is still being taught today as it was in the past. The results are the same: some children excel, but many never seem to get it right and they hate every moment of it!

Children are taught to write at an age when their motor control is sufficient for them to hold a pen properly and coordinate its movements (Fig. 287). Why then should learning to write be so difficult and unpleasant? The answer: children, too, are people, with personalities that the commonly taught methods of penmanship deny. They're forced to emulate traits that aren't necessarily their own, so there's a lot of room for improvement in teaching this subject. For example, many standard script alphabets (Fig. 288) unwittingly incorporate negative personality traits such as

**287**. *This child, age 6, is just learning how to write.*

jealousy and argumentativeness. Eventually, kids will discard such behavior if it's not part of their true nature, but how much easier for everyone if these habits didn't have to be reckoned with unnecessarily.

By contrast, a script system developed by Dr. Richard Stoller, a graphologist and psychologist, consciously tries to promote positive traits in children in teaching them how to write. In devising the chart, Dr. Stoller removed negative trait strokes, such as jealousy loops, so that only positive traits remain (Fig. 289). Dr. Stoller reports excellent results in children who've learned penmanship with this method.

Unlike the many teachers in Europe who are required to study handwriting analysis, teachers in America are generally dogmatic about teaching penmanship. For one thing, boys, even in today's liberated climate, are given greater leeway than girls, who are *expected* to have better handwriting.

Graphologically, there's no inherent difference between handwriting of males and females. Yet messiness in boys' script is tolerated more than in girls' because of cultural conditioning. Boys are not only permitted to express their energy more than girls in the classroom, but they simply aren't geared toward good penmanship.

As part of our culture, historically women have been encouraged to write beautifully. Beautiful penmanship was part of a woman's accomplishments. Before World War I, when communicating was done chiefly by letter and women were not yet part of the work force, they developed studied scripts as an art form (Fig. 290).

Modern grade school teachers often provide good examples of studied writing. They seem to have similar script not only because they teach penmanship but because they are practiced at writing impeccably on the blackboard.

## PALMER METHOD

**288.** *Some of the standard teaching alphabets in use today*

*Handwriting*

BY

**PARKER ZANER BLOSER**

*Aaa Bbb Ccc Ddd Eee Fff Ggg*
*Hhh Iii Jjj Kkk Lll Mmm Nnn*
*Ooo Ppp qq2 Rrr Sss Ttt Uuu Vvv*
*Www Xxx Yyy Zzz 1 2 3 4 5 6 7 8 9 10*

*The ability, or lack of ability, to write a*
*good business hand at a commercial rate*
*of speed may mean your success or*

**D'Nealian™ Cursive Alphabet**

a b c d e f g h i j k l m

n o p q r s t u v w x y z

A B C D E F G H I

J K L M N O P Q

R S T U V W X Y Z

**D'Nealian™ Numbers**

0 1 2 3 4 5 6 7 8 9

A POSITIVE TRAIT ALPHABET

A B C D E F G H I J K L M N O P Q R S
T U V W X Y Z

a b c d e f g h i j k l m n o p q r s t u v w x y z

1 2 3 4 5 6 7 8 9 0

*a A a B b b C c D d E e e F f f G g g g*
*H h h I i J j K K k L L l m m m u*
*N n u O o P p q g R r r S s s*
*T t t t U u V v W W w w X t x*
*Y y Z z*

**289**. *The Stoller alphabet reinforces positive traits.*

Another problem in teaching penmanship is that scrawled writing isn't tolerated. But as I've mentioned before, scrawled writing means thoughts come faster than the writer's ability to put them down. This is true for adults and some children. But, for the most part, children scrawl because they're not mature. In any case, they shouldn't be pressed and it shouldn't worry parents who are told their little Adam or Kenneth or Amanda or Stacy is a bright student but doesn't do well in penmanship.

I've consulted with many schools in my practice, and I recommend that children be taught what the letters look like but be allowed to write them in a way that's natural for them. However, children typically are not permitted to break away from the system until the age of ten or eleven. Then handwriting *truly* becomes brainwriting and the child's personality shines through. It's from this point for-

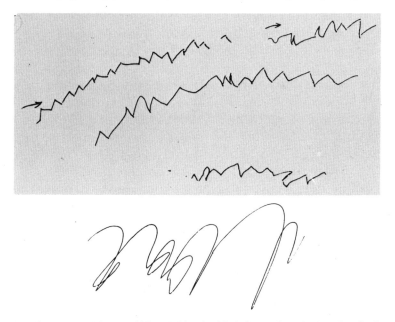

290. *In days gone by penmanship was considered an art form by many.*

291. *These prewriting scribbles yield valuable information about a developing child's character.*

ward that I personally prefer to analyze children's handwriting.

There are some traits that come through even when kids are conforming to penmanship systems. Even the prewriting scribbles of very small children show early personality trends (Fig. 291). For example, round scribbles show a developing creativity, while squares mean the child is trying to encompass an idea. Patternless scribbles indicate unorganized thinking. Often strokes such as hooks and flourishes show up and give clues. These traits give invaluable insight into a developing child's character.

### Evaluating Your Child's Handwriting

Children are little people whose uniqueness should be understood and honored. Yet often kids can't express their needs and thoughts the way adults can, so it's up to you to let their handwriting tell you what they are unable to. It's a terrific way of keeping your kids on the right track!

Because it's such a storehouse of information, you should encourage your child to write instead of print (or type), but don't force the issue, because certain personalities *need* to express themselves this way. The child who prints isn't only intuitive but wants to be clear and understood (Fig. 292).

Children are growing and maturing all the time and their handwriting shows it. But because children's handwriting is developmental, it should never be tampered with. Even the most innocent attempt to change your child's handwriting could prove harmful. With the exception of the exercise for concentration, the exercises given in *Graphotypes* shouldn't be applied to children. They're geared for adults only. Two exercises designed specifically for children are given in this chapter.

Parents and teachers who see negative traits in a child's handwriting should work with the child by giving loving guidance and counseling. The child's writing will serve as a yardstick as to whether improvements are being made or not.

All too often children are victimized by well-meaning teachers or parents who try to change the child's slant or handedness. These changes usually cause psychological problems such as severe emotional suppression. Children

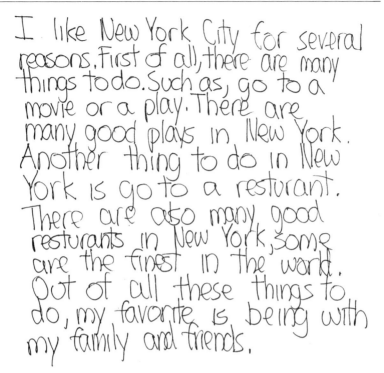

I like New York City for several reasons. First of all, there are many things to do. Such as, go to a movie or a play. There are many good plays in New York. Another thing to do in New York is go to a resturant. There are also many good resturants in New York, some are the finest in the world. Out of all these things to do, my favorite is being with my family and friends.

**292**. *This child, age 14, prints because he wants to be clear and understood.*

with backward slants, for instance, shouldn't be forced to change the slant in any way. Introtype kids who are suddenly compelled to feel extroverted emotions will be frightened and traumatized (Fig. 293). A child's Graphotype should be respected as much as an adult's.

By the same token, many left-handed children are forced to become right-handers. Handedness is related to the actual physiological/genetic structure of the body and brain, so changing handedness alters this pattern, which again proves harmful. Such is the story of one client:

When she was six, Sara Greenfield, a natural left-hander, was forced to switch to her right hand. Until this was accomplished, her left hand was physically tied behind her back so she couldn't fall back into the pattern of using it. Eventually, she learned to write with her right hand and continued this way through school. As an adult, her script exhibits two different personalities, depending on which hand does the writing (Fig. 294). Overall, she has an excessively active mind, a condition she attributes to this change.

**293**. *The slant of an Introtype child, such as this one, should never be tampered with.*

**294**. Top: *Sara's writing as a left-hander.* Bottom: *Sara's writing as a right-hander shows more of a forward slant.*

Sometimes children feel compelled to impose change on themselves. For example, the nine-year-old daughter of a friend prints in emulation of her thirteen-year-old sister, whom she envies. The older girl is a natural printer, but the younger one is really suited to script writing. Yet the nine-year-old's obsessive need overrides all else. Her parents realize they can't force her to change, but must allow her to work out her feelings naturally.

## The Parent-Child Connection

As a parent you're usually aware of the conflicts your children go through in maturing. But sometimes you can lose sight of the fact that you may be an integral part of those conflicts. Not only should you be aware of your child's temperament and needs, but you should also be self-aware and alert to the possibility that you're imposing your needs on your child.

Raising a child should really be a matter of what's right for that child, based on what his or her handwriting shows. Parents often want children to follow in their footsteps. I have counseled many of these cases, such as this one:

A prominent concert pianist, Emma de Winter, came to me highly agitated because her daughter didn't take to the piano as she desired. The girl baiked at the strict practice regimen and played poorly. Her mother was convinced the girl had talent but was deliberately playing badly out of spite. Mrs. de Winter was exasperated. Not only were her own relations with her daughter in a sorry state, but she'd received inquiries from the girl's school, where her teachers noticed a marked deterioration in attitude and schoolwork.

I saw immediately that this conflict was being imposed on the girl by the unrealistic demands of her mother. It was plain to me that the daughter simply didn't have it in her to be a concert pianist. She lacked the fluidity and interpretive skills needed for musicianship. The girl wasn't being spiteful; on the contrary, she wanted to please her mother but couldn't, which only heightened her anguish.

When I explained this to Mrs. de Winter, she was able to take a long, hard look at herself and come to terms with the situation. I pointed out that her daughter did have excellent manual dexterity (Fig. 295), but not for the piano. The child was subsequently enrolled in a pottery class where she excelled, and both mother and daughter were happy.

Parents often pressure children by demanding academic excellence in one or more subjects. Some children have no interest in academics at all and some find interest only in certain subject areas, as this case study points out:

The parents of an eleven-year-old boy were in conflict with their son, who'd become rebellious and hostile. The boy, Matthew, had always been loving and adaptable, which made his behavior seem all the more puzzling.

In our counseling session, I learned that the parents were not happy with Matthew's performance in school. They demanded straight A's in all subjects, but Matthew's work in math and science was poor. His report card frequently read: "This child is an excellent student, but shows laziness in mathematics and science work." Naturally, this assumption on the teacher's part made Matthew's parents all the more outraged.

My friends are veronica
Nell Jasmine and a lot
more We all have so
much fun together.

**295.** *Manual dexterity is evident in the rounded* m's *and flat-toppped* r's.

In point of fact, Matthew was an intelligent boy, but he simply didn't have an aptitude for math or science. His parents and teacher wrongly assumed that because he was bright he'd excel in every subject. His so-called laziness was misperceived, for his real problem stemmed from the conflict he felt in trying to please his parents.

The pressure Matthew felt was shown in his writing (Figs. 296, 297). His usual Supratype slant became very erratic, reflecting his panic and hysteria. Matthew needed to slow down, so I prescribed the following exercise:

*I went to the lake last week and went swimming for most of the day.*

296. Matthew's usual way of writing

*I had verry good time at camp, but I sure did not like the chors, we went on the sled that . . . Lera and d took. And we had hat choclat. We went on a ghost hike and we got all wet. We went for a hike with*

297. Matthew's tension and anxiety are evident in this sample, which shows erratic writing.

*SEDATIVE EXERCISE FOR CHILDREN*

Give the child a blank unlined piece of paper and allow him or her to choose a writing implement. Have the child fill up the page with the *e*-like pattern pictured in figure 298. Put some variety into the exercise by having the child use different media, such as finger paints, sand, or crayons. Repeat this exercise as needed.

**298.**

Matthew's story points out an important fact: teachers also impose their biases on children. One way this is seen is in thinking patterns. For example, teachers with fast thinking patterns often have no patience for—and do not tolerate—children with slower thinking abilities.

Many children with slow thinking patterns have been mistakenly judged as "dumb," when in reality they either need time to digest information (Fig. 299) or have bona fide learning disabilities. Unfortunately, these children often become severely frustrated because they're not understood.

Teachers can be unaware in other ways. For instance, Marge Jackson, a Supratype with an artistic flair and genuine talent for drawing, was given the opportunity to take a calligraphy class in high school. Unfortunately, what should have been an exciting learning experience turned

*I love school because of all my wonderful friends*

*I am going to walk to the store which is four blocks away.*

*My favorite animal is the tiger. I like the tiger because it is powerful.*

**299.** *These children are all methodical thinkers. They reach conclusions by building fact on fact, but may need time to do it.*

into a disappointment. Although she could form the actual calligraphic letters perfectly, she couldn't get them to lean over in the italic scripts her teacher required (Fig. 300). Her Supratype personality couldn't be forced to enter the Supratype Plus or Extrotype range.

Marge's teacher, unaware of the real nature of her problem, saw only that she wasn't getting it right, so she was graded poorly. Unfortunately, neither the teacher nor Marge at the time was aware of the psychology of handwriting.

Children should be self-aware. Parents should help younger kids understand themselves through the insights they've gained from handwriting analysis. As children grow older, they can be encouraged to study their handwriting on their own.

"Every cloud has a silver lining."
— Longfellow

".....Lizzy, our 'O', had some homework to do....."
— Shel Silverstein
Where the Sidewalk Ends

*abcdefghijkl*

*Forever is a*

**300.** Top: *Marge's natural handwriting.* Bottom: *An example of calligraphic script.*

This is especially beneficial for young adults who are graduating from high school and choosing a vocation or are preparing to enter college. High school guidance counselors have used handwriting analysis to help kids plan their futures. This case study is typical:

Jared Powell always excelled in English. He enjoyed writing and worked on his high school newspaper. As a junior, he was ready to start applying to colleges and universities and make a career choice. He'd pretty much decided to major in English and become a novelist, but his guidance counselor saw other factors through his handwriting (Fig. 301).

P.G. Wodehouse is one of my
favorite authors. Jeeves is
constantly trying to get Bertie
going in or out of jams.

**301.** *Jared Powell's handwriting shows much imagination and a need for change and variety (all seen in the inflated lower loops), which preclude a career as a novelist.*

For one thing, Jared needed to be around people. He didn't have the personality to sit alone and write all day. He also had excellent business aptitudes, so he was counseled to major in business administration and minor in English.

Jared also wasn't sure which college he'd choose. He'd considered both a college in rural Pennsylvania and a university in the Boston area. Again, his guidance counselor was able to direct him. She saw that Jared needed a lot of change and variety. She felt the city university would give Jared the stimulation his personality needed to flourish.

This kind of evaluation and guidance can help get a young adult on the right track at the outset.

Handwriting analysis has also been used on the college level in admissions and placement offices. Admissions administrators are anxious to select the right students for their school, especially where scholarships are concerned. Using graphology ensures that both student and school will be mutually satisfied. And, of course, placement offices use graphology to match the right person to the right job, in ways I've already discussed throughout this book.

## Kid Stress

Children experience stress just as adults do. Only children usually don't understand their drives and motives and may not be aware of what it is they are going through. It is up to you as a parent to understand how stress affects your children. When you're aware of your child's stress level, and what it is that the child can and can't handle, you'll be prepared for all contingencies. Knowing how a child will respond can prevent many conflicts. For example, if your child writes with heavy pressure and is an Introtype, he or she will be significantly affected by stressful situations (Fig. 302).

**302**. *This child is under severe stress.*

Children need outlets for stress such as physical activity or games and play that please them. They should also be allowed to express themselves in any nondestructive way that satisfies them. Permitting children to choose their own clothes, for instance, or decorate their own rooms, especially if you notice heavy pressure in their writing, which indicates a good color sense, are two excellent ways that allow them to expend their energy positively.

The following exercise is similar to the sedative exercise and can be used in conjunction with it to help loosen up children and alleviate anxieties:

## CALMING EXERCISE FOR CHILDREN

Follow the directions given for the sedative exercise previously demonstrated. Instead of the written *e* formations, have the child draw waves, as pictured in figure 303.

Both the calming and sedative exercises are excellent for siphoning off stress in children. They also help build a sense of harmony and fluidity.

303.

### Some Specific Evaluations of Children's Writing

All of the phases of childhood show up in children's handwriting—jealousies, sibling rivalries, lying, deceptions, and so on. Yet these generally are stages that we hope will disappear as the child matures and develops confidence.

It is necessary to approach a child's writing in the context of the child's stage of growth (Fig. 304). Adult standards can't be applied.

Sometimes, parents are unable to relate to their children, perhaps because these parents are Introtypes, for example (Fig. 305). But if a parent can't draw a child out psychologically, he or she can at least observe the child's interests and needs and still provide the direction needed.

Children need goals of their own for fulfillment. But a child's goals aren't the same as an adult's goals, which are typically "important" and viewed as long range. Children want immediacy and so their goals should be simple and short-term.

**A**

Football is a hard hitting exciting game. It's played on a 100 yard field where two teams meet and

**B**

I once, punched a kid for teasing me, He was very upset, I felt good at first but then I felt lousy, I knew I shouldnt of hit him I decided to appologize and he accepted.

**C**

I like to play in the loft. It is fun. We played monopoly in the loft, I win all the time.

**D**

Jen is too short for Nina but I don't care, I still love ballet though.

**304.** *The handwriting of children of various ages:* A: *a boy, age 15,* B: *a boy, age 8,* C: *a girl, age 9,* D: *a girl, age 11*

**305.** *Introtype parents, such as this one, may not be able to relate to children but can observe interests and needs.*

Children who have goals are motivated children and, in my experience, are generally happy, open, and satisfied. The child's goals should center on his or her interests and abilities and should allow the child to have something to look forward to. As a result, the child will feel pleased at doing something he or she can relate to and excel at.

Well-directed children who are motivated to achieve within their abilities are able to get involved in a variety of interests and relate easily to others, provided other characteristics in the handwriting support this. Children who have good goal placement are more able than others to hurdle the rough spots and overcome negativities they may be experiencing.

If the child's writing shows well-placed goals to begin with, he or she may need little more than direction into the appropriate outlet or area of interest (Fig. 306). Kids whose goal orientation is low need more support (Fig. 307). These children are like fish floundering on dry land. Parents and teachers should especially understand and guide them into an appropriate area of interest.

Goals for children are especially important when a mother decides to go to work. Unfortunately, many working mothers feel tremendous guilt about their decision to pursue a career (Fig. 308). They may doubt that they can be good mothers and hold a job as well.

*I am very happy to meet you. I have a lot of questions to ask you. Like do you like being a senator. Is it fun? Do you always get your way when*

**306.** *This child's goals are well placed.*

*I am not sure about what I want to do*

**307.** *The low t bars indicate that this child's goals aren't well placed.*

*"Suited for? What is your first choice? Second choice? Third choice? Fourth choice? Currently I am an accounting manager. It's O.K. but I*

**308.** *The back-to-self strokes indicate this mother feels guilt about returning to work.*

So much of this guilt could be eliminated if mothers would realize that children with their own goals are well adjusted. A working mother should consider her own goals and what they are meant to accomplish while also considering the experiences of her child. In other words, her child should accomplish something, too.

Yet the process of maturation isn't easy, even with strong goals in place. Usually, along the road of development many undesirable traits come and go from a child's handwriting. It's not uncommon to see these traits in children's handwriting at some stage or another:

309. Stubbornness *Aent A*

310. Procrastination *procrastination*

311. Self-consciousness *looking at me*

312. Selfishness *compressed strokes + narrow e's + initial hooks*

313. Resentment *Resentment*

314. Defiance *talk back*

315. Argumentativeness *pick a fight*

316. Dependency *soft s + low goals (t)*

317. Withdrawal *backward slant*

Fear traits often appear, especially when major traumas such as divorce or death of a parent enter a child's life. Fear can also be caused by other factors, such as fear of failure, which often stems from the child's need to please his or her parents. Such traits include:

318. Jealousy *many have more than me*

319. Repression *retraced is repression*

320. Timidity *repression + low t bars +/small Capitals*

321. Self-castigation *self castigation*

322. Sensitivity *sensitivity (t)*

The dependency trait illustrated in figure 316 is common in young children. It should be watched for in the writing of older children and adolescents who ought to be breaking away.

Severe problems in children can be shown in a number of ways. Rebelliousness and a lack of respect for authority is seen in the highly inflated loop of the letter *k* (Fig. 323).

A dented loop (Fig. 324) indicates you should look further into the child's emotional stability. Self-consciousness is shown when the second hump of the wedge in *m*'s and *n*'s is higher than the first (Fig. 325). Excessive ornamentation and flourishes in the handwriting may be a mask for insecurities (Fig 326). The child covers up feelings of inadequacy with traits of showmanship. Check the writing for other traits supportive of insecurity, such as low *t* bars or a high degree of aggressiveness (Fig. 327).

323. *k*

324. *dented loop*

325. *Must I go, Mother?*

326. *my name is Kevin*

327. *low t bars + breakaway lower loops*

328. *last week we went to the movies with my aunt*

Small handwriting, which in an adult indicates an ability to concentrate, can, in children, show that the child is living under the burden of unnatural tension. In figure 328 the script is very tiny and cramped. An example of this was shown to me by a woman I counseled:

Lisa Fields was the second child of strict parents who adhered to very dogmatic religious beliefs. Both she and her sister were expected to behave in ways that were consistent with their parents' philosophies. They attended church several times a week, studied hard, and didn't date boys. When Ms. Fields went away to college she chose a city university. Eventually, she blossomed into her own personality, enjoying interests previously closed off to her by her parents.

When I saw Ms. Fields, she was a successful executive in the fashion industry. Her handwriting was very expressive and full (Fig. 329). She also brought along a sample of a letter she had written as a child. By contrast, the script was very tiny and cramped, reflecting the burden imposed on her naturally open temperament by rigid parents (Fig. 330).

**329**. *Lisa Field's open, adult handwriting*

**330**. *The cramped, tight writing of her teen-age years*

The child who is a loner and who may be distrustful of others often shows clannishness in his or her handwriting (Fig. 331). In adults, clannishness shows a tendency to associate with a very select group of people, often those with whom one shares a common background. In children, the trait takes on an introverted aspect and the child's select circle is restricted to himself or herself. Check to see if the child is an Introtype also.

The need for attention in children often produces a cutup or "class clown" type. This may be especially pronounced if the child is an Extrotype (Fig. 332).

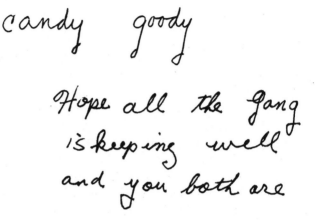

**331**. *The tiny loop at the end of the lower Graphozone stem (downstroke) indicates clannishness.*

**332**. *The desire for attention is shown by the upswung, curving final.*

## The Evaluation Process

Combinations of traits in children often produce certain types or modes of behavior, such as:

*high p stem*          *p loop full*

**333**. *argumentativeness*          + *physical activity*

The *pugnacious* child shows argumentativeness coupled with a lot of physical activity.

*backward slant*          *looped o*          *closed circle letters*

**334**. *backward slant*          + *secretiveness*          + *reticence*

The *introverted* child has a backward slant and traits of secretiveness and reticence.

*forward slant*          *good lower loops*          *open a's, o's*

**335**. *forward slant*          + *imagination*          + *talkativeness*

The *extroverted* child has a forward slant plus traits such as talkativeness and imagination.

*Extrotype*          **heavy pressure**          *very large loops*

**336**. *Extrotype*          + *heavy pressure*          + *active imagination*

The *hyperactive* child is an Extrotype who writes with heavy pressure and has an active imagination. He or she needs outlets to siphon off the excessive energy.

*weak finals*          *soft strokes*          *repression low goals*

**337**. *indecisiveness*          + *yieldingness*          + *timidity*

The *shrinking violet* shows indecisiveness, yieldingness, and timidity.

**338.** *floating t bar*

*Daydreamers* have floating *t*-bar formations with no action traits (such as persistence) that permit dreams to be put into action. Such behavior is also perceived as laziness.

*Big fast writing*      *erratic*      *poor detail orientation*

**339.** *inability to concentrate*      + *lack of rhythm*      + *poor detail orientation*

*Restless* children show an inability to concentrate, a lack of rhythm, and the inability to handle details.

*caution*      *round m or n or h*

**340.**      *caution*      + *methodical thinking pattern*

The *cautious* child shows the caution trait but may also show slow thought processes.

*lower loop breakaway*      *argumentative*      *large p loop*

**341.** *aggressiveness*      + *defensiveness*      + *physical activity*

The *overly aggressive* child, also referred to as a bully, shows aggressiveness, defensiveness, and physical activity. These children may also be domineering or have fear traits which they compensate for in their aggressive behavior.

*short t's, d's*      *high goals: t*      *Large Capitals*      *some tall t's, d's*      *firm endings*

**342.** *independence*      + *self-confidence*      + *pride*      + *decisiveness*

Children who are *independent* show this trait plus self-confidence, pride, and decisiveness.

*large k buckle*      *backward slant*      *short t's, d's*

**343.**      *defiance*      + *self-interest*      + *independence*

The child who *does as he pleases* has the traits of independence plus defiance and possibly self-interest.

*M, n, m*     *small writing*     *balanced f*

**344.** *well-developed thinking patterns*    *+ concentration*    *+ organization*

*well-dotted i's*     *retraced p*

*+ detail orientation*    *+ little need for physical activity*

Some children are *scholars*. They have well-developed thinking patterns, concentration, organization, detail orientation, and seemingly little need for physical activity.

*wedges: m, n*     *clear, wide e's*

**345.** *investigative thinking patterns*    *+ broad-mindedness*

The child filled with *curiosity* has investigative thinking patterns and broad-mindedness.

**346.** *flying t bars + self-deceit*    *t*    *looped e or ea*

The child who *shuns reality* shows flying *t* bars and self-deceit.

*t, p*     *final brought back high*

**347.** *temper traits*     *+ need for attention*

The child who throws *temper tantrums* shows temper traits—ticks, temper *t* bar—plus a need for attention.

*good loops*   *figure 8 g*   *round m's*

*heavy pressure*    *broken letters*   *flat n's*

**348.** *depth + imagination + intuition + fluidity + manual dexterity*

The *artistic child* shows depth, imagination, intuition, fluidity, and manual dexterity.

**349.** *repression + secrecy*    *retracing*    *looped o*

The child who *hides his or her true feelings* shows repression and secrecy.

**350.** *forward slant*    *forward slant*

The child who is *demonstrative* has a forward slant and no indications of timidity, secrecy, or deceit.

# 8 Getting Along: Compatibility

As social beings we deal with our fellow humans on many levels every day. We try to get along as best we can; we strive for compatibility. Sometimes we don't always achieve it, for a variety of reasons.

Compatibility is valued in all areas of life but most especially in close, interpersonal relationships, such as marriage, love, and family. Friendship and career relationships are also extremely important. Of secondary value are relationships with neighbors, passing acquaintances, and those people we come into contact with on a regular, if largely impersonal, basis, such as tradesmen or merchants.

Although we may put greater effort into getting along with the people nearest to us, the traits that allow for successful interpersonal relationships work in all situations. Of course, no two people are *exactly* alike, but well-developed positive traits can help surmount any obstacles and allow people to transcend their differences and get along.

Reaching out and maintaining bonds requires good social skills; the basic traits that especially help you understand and get along with others are:

351. Empathy  *+ Graphotypes, especially forward slant*

352. Broad-mindedness  *clear, wide e's*

353. Sympathy  *forward slant + generosity + openminded*

354. Generosity  *long finals*

355. Enthusiasm  *sweeping t-bar*

356. Communication/talkativeness  *talkative: open a's, o's*

357. Loyalty  *round i dot*

358. Optimism  *optimism*

359. Diplomacy  *tapering m's, n's*

360. Sense of humor  *initial flourishes, especially m's, n's*

361. Intuition  *spaces between letters*

On the other hand, if you don't have these traits in your handwriting, you'll have difficulty in mastering the skills that help establish positive relationships. Sensitivity to criticism, for example, is a trait that can undermine relationships (sometimes, however, sensitivity to criticism can spur people on because they don't want to encounter criticism again). So can any of the traits that are self-oriented, such as self-castigation, withdrawal, and self-consciousness, which cause people to take things too personally. Not all incompatibilities should be taken as personal rejections.

All of the exercises in *Graphotypes* are designed to build self-awareness and are especially good for giving you self-confidence. If you can detach yourself from feelings of being personally attacked, you're better able to reach out and understand the dynamics of your relationships, which clears the way for dealing with them positively. Of course, there are times in a relationship when you will be personally attacked. It's my experience, though, that it's the attacker who has the problems, because this kind of behavior is usually motivated by fears and insecurities.

Primarily, the negative traits that detract from or may destroy relationships are the ones that show up very strongly in a sample, overshadowing the positive ones. Some of the negative traits to look for in assessing compatibility are:

362. Temper *temper*

363. Deception *double loops*

364. Withdrawal *backward slant*

365. Impatience *slashed forms: i´, k*

366. Shallowness *shallow: t*

367. Selfishness *compressed strokes + narrow i's + initial hooks*

368. Narrow-mindedness *closed letters: a's, o's, e's*

369. Jealousy *small initial loops: m, n, H, B*

370. Secretiveness *looped o*

371. Evasiveness *hook in circle letter: a*

372. Vanity *extra tall t's*

373. Domineering *arrow t bar*

## Personal Compatibility

The relationships that affect us the most are our close, personal ones. We all want them to work. And of these, usually our biggest quest in life is in finding the perfect mate or lover.

How do you do it? It's not the intention or purpose of this book to advise you how to meet people, but I can tell you when you do connect with someone his or her handwriting can show you if he or she is the one for you. Then the choice is yours. If both your handwritings show compatibility, so much the better, and you can hone your relationship by being aware of what both of you share or don't share.

If the person you're interested in has handwriting that isn't compatible with yours, you have a decision to make. If you decide to continue the relationship, at least you'll be aware of what you're getting into. Sometimes you can work around profound differences, especially if *both* of you are aware and willing to understand and deal with them.

Many incompatibilities can be overcome by understanding and compromise, but some cannot. There are relationships in which the people concerned are so disparate that getting along is nearly impossible. Such was the case of a woman who was about to be married:

Evelyn Pierce, a woman in her late twenties, had been dating Greg Ademian, a bachelor in his early thirties, for over a year. Since the relationship seemed stable, Ms. Pierce, who was not only a liberated woman, but a little bit afraid that marriage would pass her by, suggested marriage to Mr. Ademian. Ms. Pierce believed she was in love. Mr. Ademian was poised and sophisticated and fun to be with. Above all else, he had a sense of humor that kept her entertained and amused. Their physical relationship was excellent, and so she believed he would make an ideal husband.

Mr. Ademian didn't resist the idea of marriage. Rather, he went along with her suggestion, possibly because he felt that at that stage of his life he should settle down.

Both samples of writing (Figs. 374, 375) were brought to me by Ms. Pierce's mother, a wonderfully perceptive woman who feared her daughter was making the wrong move. She told me Mr. Ademian seemed nice enough, but she felt something was amiss. She was right. The handwritings showed gross incompatibilities that would inevitably lead to unhappiness and divorce.

*the fid not too funny looking — although everyone says she's very cute — OK — Guess this is enough.*

**374.** *Ms. Pierce's handwriting with its forward slant*

*Mary is coming to my house*

**375.** *Mr. Ademian's writing*

Ms. Pierce's handwriting showed that she was a basically warm, outgoing person. As an Extrotype, she was naturally expressive and had a large capacity to empathize. She was also talkative, imaginative, and needed to be noticed and paid attention to (Fig. 376).

On the other hand, Mr. Ademian was an Introtype. He was generally introverted and self-centered, with an inability to show deep affection or emotion. His sample (Fig. 377) also showed traits of jealousy and secretiveness. There were some very positive traits, too, such as dignity, loyalty, and frankness, but they still weren't enough to compensate for what Ms. Pierce really wanted. She needed a husband who would communicate his feelings and pay a great deal of attention to her and socialize with many people. Mr. Ademian lacked all of these attributes. His humor and sophistication were smokescreens for his introverted character. He was essentially a loner who preferred superficial encounters of his choosing.

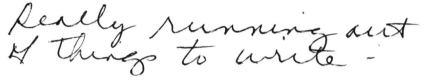

376. *The full lower loops show a need to socialize with many people.*

377. *Dignity is shown by the retraced* d, *but the lack of lower* g *loop shows a loner.*

Unfortunately, Ms. Pierce's vision was clouded, and she deeply resented her mother's interference. Ms. Pierce and Mr. Ademian were married but divorced four years later. Ms. Pierce discovered that what she initially found attractive in Mr. Ademian ultimately wasn't enough to fulfill her needs.

Had these two unfortunate people been aware of the value of handwriting analysis, by exercising their options they might have saved themselves the trauma of a bad marriage and its subsequent breakup. They might have remained friends, or they might have broken up, or Mr. Ademian might have decided to seek therapy and reach out of himself.

Empathy, which was one of Mr. Ademian's greatest deficiencies, is extremely important in relationships. Empathy, shown in your emotional responsiveness, is the basis for understanding. Practice the empathy exercise in Chapter

6 if you want to improve the quality of your relationships. Intuition goes hand in hand with empathy and is another major ingredient in your ability to establish compatible relationships. Intuitive people are sensitive to the makeup, temperament, needs, and abilities of others, and understand what they may be going through. Intuition can be heightened and developed by practicing the following exercise:

## EXERCISE FOR IMPROVING INTUITION

On a page of legal-size paper write the word *intuition* over and over again down half the page. Then fill up the rest of the page with a short sentence containing *intuition*. Only this time, make breaks between the letters—as many as you can handle (Fig. 378). Do this exercise for two days.

378.

When you feel you are ready, culminate your practice by using your intuition to direct you to new contacts. For example, if you are at a business meeting or social function, approach someone in a crowd who you think might be helpful to you or whom you might be compatible with. Base your approach to them on your intuition. Carefully observe if your perceptions about the person were right or not.

Of course, self-awareness is also a major component in getting along with others and, for the most part, people *choose* their relationships, so it's important to try to make correct choices. Obviously, correct choices lead to compatible relationships, while incorrect ones produce conflicts. True compatibility boils down to a shared commonality of traits, with an ability to bridge whatever differences there are with understanding. Such is the case with these two people:

Jennifer Ryan and John Braebeck were high school sweethearts who assumed they'd eventually marry. But each went to a different college, and Mr. Braebeck served a hitch in the army after that. They drifted apart and lost contact. Eventually, Mr. Braebeck married, had children, and divorced.

Some years later, Mr. Braebeck and Ms. Ryan resumed their relationship, which, with maturity, was fuller and better than ever, except for one obstacle. Ms. Ryan, who'd never been married, resented Mr. Braebeck's previous marriage and two children. She was aware of this and saw this trait in her handwriting (Fig. 379). Mr. Braebeck sensed her resentment and was upset by it, but he understood and made an effort to make allowances (Fig. 380). Both were able to communicate their feelings, and through discussion, the couple worked out their problem.

*Photography has always been extremely important to me — I think it is the process of creating beauty and harmony in the universe which appeals to me most.*

**379.** *The approach strokes that come up from the base line and lean against letter forms indicate resentment in Ms. Ryan's sample.*

Fortunately, both these people were aware and honest with each other, and they have a very successful marriage. Had they not been able to empathize, the relationship may well have been unsuccessful, or ended.

Sometimes we don't have a choice in selecting the people we associate with. Such is the case with family members, as this example points out:

*And, yes, he's hoping to be here around the 28th of Sept.*

**380**. *Mr. Braebeck's forward-slanting writing shows empathy and intuition (in the breaks between letters).*

Richard and David Fine were two brothers in their late teens who seemed never to get along. After putting up with years of bickering, their parents came to me as a last resort. The boys' handwriting did indeed show much incompatibility (Figs. 381, 382), but I knew there was an option, even though it wasn't immediately apparent.

*last few courses were very tedious drafting & rendering projects — drawing things to*

**381**. *Richard Fine's creativity is seen in the well-developed lower loops.*

I met with both boys and their parents in a counseling session and probed to find a common denominator. I'd seen that Richard was artistic and intuitive, while David was scientifically inclined. We discovered an area of interest that

*Thanks for your help. The article appears on page 48.*

**382.** *David Fine's scientific ability can be seen, in part, by the retraced p, which shows precision.*

appealed to both of them—photography. Richard began taking pictures and David developed them. Sharing a common interest helped bring them closer together and alleviated the tension.

What this story brings out, and the main thing to remember when you're in a relationship you didn't choose, is that there are always options.

### Compatibility on the Job

Your work life puts you in contact with people you spend a great deal of time with—thirty-five hours a week on the average, or about half of your waking hours! Naturally, you want to get along with those you work with, work for, or have work for you.

In my business I analyze the handwriting of everyone I have dealings with to make sure we have the best relationship possible. Happiness on your job depends not only on your being satisfied with what you do but on your getting along with the people you come into contact with. A bad relationship in your work can cause stress and dampen your enthusiasm and efficiency.

Again, the best way to handle incompatibilities at work —as anywhere—is to get a handle on what makes the other person function and understand his or her motivations.

The following is a case in point:

A secretary, Jean Scouras, came to me with a sample of her boss's handwriting. She essentially loved her job but found it difficult to work for this man. Ms. Scouras worked hard, but felt she wasn't being appreciated. Indeed, I saw a lot of sarcasm and criticism in his writing (Fig. 383). Under the circumstances, I counseled Ms. Scouras to find an option. Subsequently, she was able to transfer to another job within her company, with her boss's permission.

**383.** *The inflated d's in Ms. Scouras's sample of her boss's writing show sensitivity to criticism; unfortunately, she was working for a highly critical individual.*

Here's a similar problem from another point of view and with another outcome:

An executive client sent me the writing sample of his secretary, whom he was about to fire. I knew the woman in question, an intelligent, proficient, poised individual with excellent skills. They'd been working together for six months and everything appeared to be running smoothly. But an examination of both their samples revealed the basic difference and source of incompatibility was in their thinking patterns (Figs. 384, 385).

**384.** *The needlepoints in the executive's handwriting show him to be a rapid thinker.*

**385.** *The rounded letters* m *and* n *in this sample show the secretary to be a methodical thinker.*

The needlepoints in the employer's handwriting showed an ability to think and assimilate information rapidly, while rounded *m*'s and *n*'s in the secretary's writing indicated a need to assimilate information slowly and methodically. The executive had no idea they each thought differently; he assumed that everyone thought essentially the same way, and so as fast as he finished his work, he gave it to her to process.

The constant deluge of work panicked and overwhelmed her. As a result, she felt pressured into producing very quickly, so in turn, the quality of her work began to decline, putting her job in jeopardy.

My client didn't want to lose a good secretary and he was delighted to find out there were options open for both of them. One solution was to allow her to work for someone low key, like herself. Another was to hire a temporary secretary one day a week to help with the output, and a third option, which the boss took, was to stagger her work load. So, even though his work was complete, it didn't actually turn up on her desk all at once. Instead, the work was doled out in batches the secretary could easily handle without panicking. The executive found this acceptable, and the secretary found it a relief.

The solution worked because each became aware of the differences in the other and was able to work around them. Had I not intervened, and had handwriting analysis not been used as a means of gaining insight into the problem, a very good secretary would have been fired. Instead, an apparent incompatibility was understood, dealt with, and reversed.

Often, I'm called upon to put together business teams, such as the sales force I created for *Working Woman* magazine, and to consult in matters of partnerships, mergers, and acquisitions. These are generally high powered and important business deals in which much is at stake. Money is a powerful incentive to form workable partnerships and close deals quickly and efficiently.

But no amount of money can ensure the success of a partnership. If the people involved aren't compatible, personality conflicts will eventually undermine the success of any venture. With so much at stake, it behooves companies and entrepreneurs alike to see if the individuals involved mesh well and can be productive together. I've saved many companies and individuals significant time and money by analyzing compatibility.

I've also been associated with companies that perform the service of matching business partners on all levels. Naturally, a business that exists to provide such a service must have a success record, and that's where my expertise comes in.

The following two case studies are excellent examples of how handwriting analysis is used in this regard:

Introduced at a convention, Harvey Roberts and Jack Heath formed an instant liking for each other. Each owned a commercial real-estate business in the same metropolitan area, and they soon decided to join forces.

In the beginning, the business flourished. The men seemed to complement each other quite well. Mr. Roberts was outgoing and lively. He was appealing to customers and made many important sales contacts (Fig. 386). Mr. Heath was far more reserved, presenting an image of dignity and confidence (Fig. 387). This was also attractive to customers, who felt their affairs were in capable, steady hands.

Eventually, though, the men began to get on each other's nerves. Mr. Roberts began to resent what he thought was

386. *The Extrotype handwriting of Mr. Roberts*

*We not only added to our knowledge but also reinforced what we already knew. At the breakfasts and dinners we learned how*

**387**. *Mr. Heath is a Supratype.*

Mr. Heath's indifference, and Mr. Heath, although truly appreciative of Mr. Roberts's efforts, didn't realize he wasn't giving him the feedback he needed. Mr. Heath also had to admit that at times Mr. Roberts's extroversion was irritating to him.

The rift between the two widened and the business began to fail. It was at this point that I was called in by Mr. Roberts with Mr. Heath's full consent.

The emotional responsiveness between Mr. Roberts and Mr. Heath was different enough to cause these misunderstandings. Mr. Roberts was an Extrotype who needed to be reassured, while Mr. Heath, a Supratype, simply didn't realize he should be more communicative with his partner. Each one, in his own way, was a valuable component of the business because each had his own unique talent to contribute. But on a personal level, their fundamental disparity got the better of them. Fortunately, counseling gave them the understanding they needed to resume their partnership, and with this insight the business and friendship thrived.

The second case study involves two women who were about to enter a partnership:

Sheryl Brill and Ann Kaplan were middle-aged businesswomen who'd known each other professionally. They both had the same desire—to go into business for themselves—so they decided to open a clothing store. With each planning session they grew to like each other even more, and a strong bond of friendship formed. Yet their lawyer, a client of mine, wanted to be completely sure that their partnership would be a success and so he referred them to me. Their compatibility was evident, but I had some important suggestions that were vital to their future business.

Both handwritings showed similar Graphotypes: Ms. Brill being an Extrotype (Fig. 388) and Ms. Kaplan a Supratype Plus (Fig. 389), so their emotional responsiveness was compatible. They also shared common interests and goals. But some specific trait patterns were different enough to be potentially troublesome. For instance, Ms. Brill's handwriting showed sensitivity to criticism (Fig. 390), while Ms. Kaplan's showed a tendency for perfectionism. Ms. Brill's also indicated immediacy, while Ms. Kaplan's had procrastination (Fig. 391).

388. *The Extrotype slant of Ms. Brill's writing indicates immediacy.*

389. *The consistency and even spacings in Ms. Kaplan's writing shows her perfectionism.*

*Setting up a designer's corner will be exiting*

**390**. Ms. Brill's inflated d loops also show a sensitivity to criticism.

*Were mentioned.*
*Within several weeks I will have completed a*

**391**. The t bar crossed to the left only indicates Ms. Kaplan's tendency to procrastinate.

In a close working relationship, it would have been all too easy for Ms. Brill to misconstrue Ms. Kaplan's perfectionism as a personal criticism of her work or style, while Ms. Brill's need to have things done immediately could have worn on Ms. Kaplan, who would be content to let things go for a while.

Alerted to the potential problem spots, both Ms. Brill and Ms. Kaplan entered into their partnership with great enthusiasm, and their clothing store subsequently blossomed.

Compatibility studies through handwriting analysis can be applied to any situation. The scope is unlimited: whenever people interact with other people, compatibility is the goal and handwriting analysis is the means to achieve that goal.

In fact, this entire book has been about compatibility: between individuals and between groups of people, between the individual and his or her environment, and between individuals and their own goals, whether they be in career situations, parenting, or intimate relationships. If compatibility can be described as the ability to live in the world in a state of harmony with others and with self, then handwriting analysis is the ideal way to achieve it.

## The Evaluation Process

Characteristics that influence relationships can be found when certain traits are shown together, such as:

*initial hooks*               *arrow X bar*

**392**. *acquisition*               + *domineering*

The *demanding* person has both acquisition and domineering traits.

*= direct: no initial strokes*   *backward slant*   *excessive flourishes*

**393**. *blunt*               + *self-interest*               + *ostentation*

*extra tall t's*   *open o's, a's*

+ *vanity*               + *talkativeness*

The *rude* individual has bluntness, self-interest, ostentation, vanity, and talkativeness.

*v forms: m, n*   *slashed forms*   *open o's, a's*   */B, /M, /H*   *arrow*   *t bar*
                  *i, k*

**394**. *analytical*     + *irritable*     + *talkative*     + *resentment*   + *sarcasm*

Those who *nag* are analytical, irritable, talkative, and show resentment and sarcasm.

*open o's, a's*   *k*   *arrow t bar*   *slashed forms: i, k*

**395**. *talkative*     + *temper*     + *sarcasm*     + *irritability*

The *perpetually scolding* person is talkative, has a temper, shows sarcasm and irritability.

*variable slant*   *confusion of interests*

**396**. *variable slant*     + *confusion*

The *fickle* individual has a variable slant and confusion.

**397.** *resentment*    + *sensitivity*    + *domineering*    + *vivid imagination*

The *antagonistic* person shows resentment and sensitivity, is domineering, and has a vivid imagination.

**398.** *active imagination*    + *talkative*    + *curiosity*    + *sarcasm*

+ *analytical thinking patterns*

The *gossip* has an active imagination, is talkative, has curiosity, and, often, has sarcasm and analytical thinking patterns.

**399.** *temper*    + *resentment*    + *sarcasm*    + *domineering*

The person who is *very demanding and gruff* has temper traits, resentment, sarcasm, and is domineering.

**400.** *domineering*    + *vanity*    + *narrow-mindedness*    + *resentment*

The *tyrannical* individual shows domination, vanity, narrow-mindedness, and, often, resentment.

**401.** *yielding*    + *indecisive*    + *self-conscious*    + *repression*

The *milquetoast* is yielding, indecisive, self-conscious, and repressed.

*open c's, o's    slashed forms: i', t'    v forms: m, n       X*

**402.** *talkative* + *irritable* + *analytical* + *domineering*

The *quarrelsome* person is talkative, irritable, analytical, and domineering; self-interest and resentment may also be present.

*forward slant           clear, wide e*

**403.** *forward slant* + *broad-minded*

The *considerate* person has a forward slant, broad-mindedness, and no indications of vanity, resentment, or domineering tendencies.

*forward slant    long finals    open circle letters    large l, g loop*

**404.** *sympathetic* + *generous* + *open-minded* + *responsible*

The *helpful* individual is sympathetic, generous, open-minded, and responsible.

*long finals    large upper loops    forward slant    open circle letters    clear, wide e*

**405.** *generous* + *philosophically oriented* + *sympathetic* + *broad-minded*

The *charitable* person is generous, philosophically oriented, sympathetic, and broad-minded.

# 9 The Graphoprofile: Your Personal Inventory

As you have been reading these chapters, you have been evaluating your own handwriting and gaining insights into your personality. Now, armed with a complete battery of information, you are about to put it all together and discover your own power potential.

Fill out the following checklist as Part One of your Graphoprofile—your own personal inventory.

**Graphoprofile**
1. My Graphotype is (found in the slant):
    Introtype
    Supratype
    Supratype Plus
    Extrotype
2. My depth (found in the pressure I write with) is:
    Heavy
    Medium
    Light

## 3. THINKING PATTERNS

| | | |
|---|---|---|
| Comprehensive/fast thinker (needlepoints) | Yes | No |
| Methodical thinker (rounded *m*'s, *n*'s) | Yes | No |
| Analytical (V formations, *m*'s *n*'s) | Yes | No |
| Investigative (wedges in *m*'s, *n*'s) | Yes | No |
| Exploratory (very deep wedges, *m*'s, *n*'s) | Yes | No |

*Supportive Traits*

| | | |
|---|---|---|
| Concentration (small writing) | Yes | No |
| Detail orientation (*i* dots) | Yes | No |
| Independent thinking (short *t*'s, *d*'s) | Yes | No |
| Intuition (breaks between letters) | Yes | No |
| Rhythm (smooth writing flow) | Yes | No |

*Reductive Traits*

| | | |
|---|---|---|
| Confusion (lower loops into next writing line) | Yes | No |
| Impulsiveness (forward slant) | Yes | No |
| Superficial thinking (ill-formed *m*'s, *n*'s) | Yes | No |

## 4. GOAL ORIENTATION

| | | |
|---|---|---|
| Visionary goals (floating *t* bar) | Yes | No |
| High goals (*t* bar rests on stem or crosses near top) | Yes | No |
| Practical goals (*t* bar crosses middle of stem) | Yes | No |
| Limited goals (*t* bar placed low) | Yes | No |
| Low goals (*t* bar crosses bottom of stem) | Yes | No |

*Achievement Traits*

| | | |
|---|---|---|
| Acquisitiveness (initial hooks) | Yes | No |
| Aggressiveness (breakaway strokes in lower loops) | Yes | No |
| Decisiveness (firm final strokes) | Yes | No |
| Directness (no initial strokes) | Yes | No |
| Enthusiasm (sweeping *t* bar) | Yes | No |
| Imagination (fullness in upper and lower loops) | Yes | No |
| Initiative (breakaway finals) | Yes | No |
| Organization (balanced *f* loops) | Yes | No |
| Persistence (tie strokes) | Yes | No |
| Precision (retraced lower *p* loop) | Yes | No |
| Tenacity (final hooks) | Yes | No |

*Reductive Traits*

| | | |
|---|---|---|
| Caution (straight finals or dashes) | Yes | No |
| Procrastination (*t* bar crossed to left of stem only) | Yes | No |

### 5. FEAR TRAITS

| | | |
|---|---|---|
| Desire for attention (finals raised high) | Yes | No |
| Indecisiveness (weak finals) | Yes | No |
| Jealousy (small initial loops, especially in *m*'s, *n*'s) | Yes | No |
| Repression (retraced strokes) | Yes | No |
| Self-castigation (pronounced back-to-self finals) | Yes | No |
| Self-conscious (second hump of *m* higher than first) | Yes | No |
| Self-underestimation (low placement of *t* bars) | Yes | No |
| Sensitivity (loops in *t* and *d* stems) | Yes | No |
| Timidity (no self-confidence, repression) | Yes | No |
| Ultraconservatism (very compressed letters) | Yes | No |
| Withdrawal (backward slant) | Yes | No |

### 6. DEFENSES

| | | |
|---|---|---|
| Bluff (exaggerated blunt downstrokes) | Yes | No |
| Narrow-mindedness (compressed *o*'s, *a*'s, *e*'s) | Yes | No |
| Perfectionism (precise letter structure and even spaces) | Yes | No |
| Reticence (closed circle letters) | Yes | No |
| Argumentative (stem of small *p* begins at point higher than the buckle) | Yes | No |
| Defiance (enlarged *k* buckle) | Yes | No |
| Irritability (slashed *i* dot) | Yes | No |
| Resentment (inflexible initial stroke drawn up from base line) | Yes | No |
| Sarcasm (arrow or knifelike *t* bar) | Yes | No |
| Stubbornness (downstroke firm, forming obtuse angle with base line) | Yes | No |
| Temper (temper tick or *t* bar to right of stem only) | Yes | No |
| Desire for variety (long broad loops) | Yes | No |

| | | |
|---|---|---|
| Vanity (tall *t* stem) | Yes | No |

## 7. INTEGRITY TRAITS

| | | |
|---|---|---|
| Ambition (high *t* bars and initial hooks) | Yes | No |
| Broad-mindedness (open *a*'s, *e*'s, *o*'s) | Yes | No |
| Conservatism (compressed letters) | Yes | No |
| Determination (long, straight downstrokes) | Yes | No |
| Dignity (retraced *t* and *d* stems) | Yes | No |
| Frankness (clean circle letters open or closed) | Yes | No |
| Loyalty (small round *i* dots) | Yes | No |
| Pride (*t* and *d* stems 2 and 2½ times height of Middle Graphozone letters) | Yes | No |
| Sincerity (round *i* dot and no deceit) | Yes | No |

*Negative Influences*

| | | |
|---|---|---|
| Deceit (double loops *a*'s and *o*'s) | Yes | No |
| Evasiveness (double hooks and tucked in hooks in circle letters) | Yes | No |
| Secretiveness (loop on inside of *o* or *a* on right side) | Yes | No |
| Self-deceit (loop on inside of *o* or *a* on left side) | Yes | No |
| Yieldingness (strokes lacking definite formation in round letters) | Yes | No |

## 8. SOCIAL TRAITS

| | | |
|---|---|---|
| Diplomacy (tapering at ends of words, especially *m*'s, *n*'s) | Yes | No |
| Generosity (long finals) | Yes | No |
| Humor (initial flourishes, any letter) | Yes | No |
| Optimism (upward slant of words, letters, or lines) | Yes | No |
| Physical mindedness (loop in *p* stem) | Yes | No |
| Self-confidence (large capital letters, high *t* bars) | Yes | No |
| Self-control (convex *t* bar) | Yes | No |
| Talkativeness (open *a*'s, *o*'s) | Yes | No |

*Negative Influences*

| | | |
|---|---|---|
| Clannishness (lower loop remote from base line and small and round) | Yes | No |
| Domination (pointed *t* bar slanting downward) | Yes | No |

| | | |
|---|---|---|
| Impatience (slashed *i* dot, impulsive slant, and forceful drives) | Yes | No |
| Ostentation (many flourishes and ornamentations throughout) | Yes | No |
| Selfishness (compressed strokes, initial hooks, and narrow *e*'s) | Yes | No |
| Shallowness (concave *t* bars) | Yes | No |

You are now ready to make an evaluation of your personality based on the information already in your notebook and what you've just checked off. Use your intuition as well as what you've learned to get an overall impression of your personality profile. Look for harmony and balance. If there is too much of any one thing, your sample shows imbalance.

Look for traits that contradict and check if controls have been developed. Remember, also, that the frequency with which traits show up is an important evaluation factor. Finally, the integration of traits is equally important. Here are some concluding examples involving Graphotypes and a reiteration of combinations already given, in equation form:

| | |
|---|---|
| *Introtype* | + clannishness = aloof |
| | + conservatism + narrow-mindedness = suspicious |
| | +depth + temper + repression + sarcasm = potentially explosive |
| | + domineering + vanity = arrogant |
| | + stubbornness = won't admit when wrong |
| | + repression + depth = stoic |
| *Supratype* | + generosity = will do things for others |
| | + dignity = formality |
| | + caution + analytical thinking = calculating |
| | + repression + timidity + secrecy + self-consciousness = inhibited |
| | + depth + self-control = temperate |
| *Supratype Plus* | + generosity − vanity = altruistic |

*Extrotype*

+ depth + enthusiasm = fervent
+ generosity + broad-mindedness +
frankness = expansive
+ responsibility + variety = a joiner
+ yieldingness + broad-mindedness =
amenable
+ enthusiasm + willpower = dynamic
+ ostentation + desire for attention =
melodramatic
+ talkativeness + imagination (much) =
blows things out of proportion
+ depth + comprehension = impressionable
+ talkativeness + desire for attention =
nonstop talker
+ optimism + light pressure = very resilient
+ temper + sensitivity = high strung
+ enthusiasm + loyalty + determination +
good goals = zealot

*Daring* = initiative + self-reliance + independence + comprehension
*Impressive* = some vanity + high goals + showmanship
*Resourceful* = initiative + analytical ability + some defiance
*Shrewd* = comprehension + imagination + analytical ability + some deceit
*Resilience* = optimism + enthusiasm + light pressure
*Dynamic* = Plus Graphotype + enthusiasm + willpower − timidity − inhibitions
*Forceful* = initiative + aggression + willpower + determination + optimism
*Enterprising* = initiative + ambition
*Accommodating* = generosity + responsibility + yieldingness − resentment − selfishness
*Go-getter* = initiative + aggression + willpower + persistence + determination + optimism

*Patient* = self-control + diplomacy + generosity + broad-mindedness − temper − irritability

*Conscientious* = loyalty + frankness + persistence − deceit

*Common sense* = practical goals + logical thinking + conservatism

*Eager to learn* = exploratory thinking patterns + enthusiasm + acquisitiveness

*Agreeable* = yieldingness − temper − irritability

*Faithful* = loyalty + honesty + open-mindedness

*Levelheaded* = cool and poised − temper

*Reliable* = loyalty + pride + persistence + determination − deceit − confusion

*Fairness* = poise + broad-mindedness − deceit

*Diligent* = persistence + detail orientation

*Foresight* = comprehension + initiative + analytical ability + intuition

*Dependable* = honesty + pride + persistence + determination + optimism − deceit

*Thorough* = detail orientation + precision + persistence + determination + tenacity

*Leadership* = comprehension + enthusiasm + pride + initiative + self-confidence − timidity − self-doubt

*Pugnacious* = argumentativeness + physical activity

*Introversion* = backward slant + secrecy + reticence

*Extroversion* = forward slant + talkativeness + imagination

*Hyperactive* = Extrotype + heavy pressure + active imagination + physical activity

*Shrinking violet* = indecisiveness + yieldingness + timidity

*Daydreamer* = floating *t* bar − action traits

*Restless* = inability to concentrate + lack of rhythm + inability to handle details

*Cautious* = caution + methodical thinking pattern

*Overly aggressive* = aggression + defensiveness + physical activity (+ sometimes domineering)

*Independent* = independence + self-confidence + pride + decisiveness

*Does as one pleases* = independence + defiance + self-interest

*Scholarly* = well-developed thinking patterns + concentration + organization + detail orientation − physical activity

*Curiosity* = investigative thinking patterns + broad-mindedness

*Shuns reality* = flying *t* bars + self-deceit

*Temper tantrums* = temper traits + desire for attention

*Artistic* = depth + imagination + intuition + fluidity + manual dexterity

*Hides true feelings* = repression + secrecy

*Demonstrative* = forward slant − timidity − deceit − secrecy

*Demanding* = acquisition + domineering

*Rudeness* = bluntness + self-interest + ostentation + vanity + talkativeness

*Nag* = analytical + irritable + talkativeness + resentment + sarcasm

*Perpetually scolding* = talkativeness + temper + sarcasm + irritability

*Fickle* = variable slant + confusion

*Antagonistic* = resentment + sensitivity + domineering + vivid imagination

*Gossip* = talkativeness + active imagination + curiosity + sarcasm + analytical ability

*Demanding and gruff* = temper traits + resentment + sarcasm + domineering

*Tyrannical* = domineering + vanity + narrow-mindedness + resentment + physical mindedness

*Milquetoast* = yieldingness + indecisiveness + self-conscious + repression

*Quarrelsome* = talkativeness + irritable + analytical + domineering + resentment + argumentative

*Considerate* = forward slant + broad-mindedness − vanity − resentment − domineering

*Helpful* = empathy + generosity + open-mindedness + responsibility

*Charitable* = generosity + philosophically oriented + empathy + broad-mindedness

Part Two of your personal inventory involves the final exercise of *Graphotypes*—and the ultimate exercise in reaching your power potential. To complete your Graphoprofile, *write a report on your findings*, or make a tape if you feel more comfortable recording them.

Choose a format that suits you, but be thorough and honest. The act of committing your analysis to paper or tape will drive home many important points about yourself. When you are finished, you should have a remarkable portrait of your own personality, and you'll have discovered your power potential. Work on weak points if you have to by going back to the exercises in this book. Utilize strengths to their maximum effectiveness. It's up to you now to choose your options and take your world by storm!

# INDEX